"

Bible Poems
for Reflection *and* Response

Bible Poems

for Reflection *and* Response

Donna Marie Merritt

Peace, Prayer, & Poetry!

Marie Merritt

Donna

CLADACH
Publishing

Dedicated to all those who have guided me on my continuing journey of faith, with a special shout-out to…

Etta Wilson
Sister Jewel Renna
Sister Judith Mulhall
Deacon George Pettinico
Deacon Neil Culhane
Father Stu Pinette
Father Jim Gregory
Father Michael Santiago

Bible Poems for Reflection and Response
© 2020 by Donna Marie Merritt

An AGATES Book of Poetry
Published by
CLADACH Publishing
Greeley, CO 80633
https://cladach.com

Cover photo by Brianna Loyot

Poems are based on the Saint Joseph Edition of the *New American Bible*, Copyright © 1996 Catholic Book Publishing.
Poems/Scriptures from Deuterocanonical (Apocryphal) Books are marked with †

ISBN: 9781945099250

Dear Reader,

Do you shy away from reading the Bible? *Bible Poems for Reflection and Response* offers a way to ease into the enduring Word of God.

Not sure if you're a poetry person? These poems are accessible—no obscure poetic language, no hidden meanings. They range from traditional rhyme to haiku to free verse. There is something for everyone and yet you will find that the poems seem to speak personally to you.

You don't have to read it in sequence. Jump around if you like. Read a poem every day, or twice a day, or once a week. This is your book to read and interpret as you like. You can read the Bible verses suggested (and beyond) or simply the poems—or both.

And because this is your book, you will find space—interspersed blank pages and wide margins—to respond to what you're reading and feeling. By adding your thoughts, prayers, reflections, poems, drawings, and doodles, this book will truly become a conversation between you and our Father.

With Peace, Prayer, and Poetry,

Donna Marie Merritt

Contents

Genesis 1; 2:1-3

THE
BEGINNING

Artist
pierces
darkness with
light
day, night

Artist
separates
water from
sky
drops, dry

Artist
moves
sea from
earth
seedlings, birth

Artist
paints
sun in
view
moon, too

Artist
fills
water and
air
life shared

Artist
creates
animals and
man
gracious plan

Artist
delights
in His best
reflects
and rests

Such is
Art ...
masterpiece
mystery
our history

Genesis 3

TEMPTATION

Man said
Wife said
Serpent said
to taste
We acted in haste
But what did You expect
Did You want us to resist
temptation?

Why did you not listen to Me?
From the garden
I must now set you free.

What?
But I told You
Wife told me
to taste
Serpent told her
to taste
It's not our fault!

Why did you not listen to Me?
From the garden,
I must now set you free.

But someone
TOLD us to do it
We cannot be blamed
Temptation is the name
Of something hideous,
Not us!
Wait, do not close the gate …
Wife, are we alone?
Must we atone
for our sins?
But it's the snake
who made us do this thing!
Isn't it?

Genesis 4:1-12

MY BROTHER'S KEEPER

Am I my brother's keeper?
Yes.

Am I responsible for him?
Yes.

Must I keep him safe?
Yes.

Violence is borne
of trivialities, differences
false righteousness
sense of entitlement

Cain murdered Abel
due to jealousy
resentment, wanting to be
the favored one

Must we protect one another?
Yes.

Should we settle differences?
Yes.

Should we strive for peace?
Yes.

Be the keeper of all mankind.

Genesis 5:3-5, 32

WHAT IS TIME?

After Abel and Cain
from Adam and Eve came
another child, Seth

Adam was strong, sturdy
One hundred thirty
when Seth was born

Adam lived another eight
hundred years after that date
to nine hundred plus

Noah was here five hundred years
when his children appeared—
Shem, Ham, Japheth …

When we contemplate
the six days to create
We must remember that

The Artist never said His power
was confined to twenty-four-hour
days to be measured as we see fit

God's time is not our time
His ways—marvelous, sublime
are not ours to know

He may have set in motion
what scientists and theologians
argue about for no reason

We can praise what God provides
without having to decide
exactly how He does it

Genesis 9:11-17

PROMISE

God cleaned house
in the time of Noah
swept our dwelling place
free of evil and debris
used plenty of water
to scrub it, make it new
to help us begin again
without all those cobwebs

And when God was done
He gave it a final polish
by adding something
spectacular, shimmering
to the sky for us to see
and consider and sigh
knowing He loves us
despite our faults, sins

We are to remember
His promise when it
appears, are to recall
His covenant with Noah
understand that never
again will God give our
world such a vigorous
spring cleaning

Genesis 11:1-9

POWER

God's children
decided they
did not
need Him
anymore

By their own   Invincible,
power they   they would
built a tower   survive, thrive
to the   without God's
firmament   guidance

God loved   He scattered   He did this
His children   them, and   so they would
too much to   their common   remember the
let them   language was   Artist and
tumble   forgotten   flourish

Genesis 12:10-20

TRUTH

sometimes

we think
a little white lie
will work to our
advantage

blink
and it changes
lies emerge
out of fear

right, Abram?

Genesis 15:2-6

FAITH

Count the grass blades
growing in yard
Too hard?

Count snowflakes
falling from sky
Can't try?

Count molecules
flying through air
Don't dare?

Yet when God told Abram
his descendants would be
as numerous as the stars
beyond what he could see,

When Abram felt his body
becoming worn and old,
when he knew Sarai's womb
was empty, growing cold,

"Abram put his faith in the Lord."

What does God whisper
when you take time to hear?
What does God tell you
when you let Him come near?

Does God lovingly confide
things you won't believe?
Does God say He's on your side?
Does God say He'll never leave?

Put your faith in the Lord.

Genesis 16:1-4

ISHMAEL

Abram and Sarai said
they believed
God's plan for them
but still thought
it best to take matters
into their own hands

Silly people

Genesis 18:1-15; 21:1-8

LAUGHTER

Sarai, now Sarah,
laughed when God's
messengers told
Abram, now Abraham,
that she would bear a child
in her old age

When Isaac was born
Sarah laughed again

Why?

I believe she laughed
the first time
because it sounded
so ridiculous
so preposterous
She, after all,
knew her body

I believe she laughed
the second time
out of pure joy
out of wonder
when she understood
that God's tenderness
has no boundaries

Do we laugh
at God
or
with God?

Do we recognize
joy and wonder
and tenderness
and understand
that God is trying
to share all this
with His children?

Genesis 19:12-26

JUST LIKE THAT

Running for her *life*
That's what Lot's wife
was doing

But was their old life
really that horrible?
Surely things had not
been that bad

She stopped moving
forward, looked back
In an instant, she was
locked inside
a pillar of salt

Her choices were gone
In that single moment
she lost the ability
to start a new life

Heart pounding
hurrying with husband
trailing two daughters
Fleeing evil

But she had trouble
leaving her old life
completely behind
even for the sake
of her family

Running for *her* life
That's what Lot's wife
was doing

Genesis 22:1-3

READY

God called to Abraham
Abraham said, "Ready!"
God called to Abraham
to sacrifice his son Isaac

I wonder if Abraham
wavered for a moment
was sick to his stomach
wished he hadn't answered
quite so quickly

When God calls us
Do we say
we are ready?
Or do we ask God
what He wants first
so we can ponder it?

"I'll do whatever
You want, Lord"
(as long as
it is not too hard
and not too long
and will not
inconvenience me)

At times our Father
asks of us things
we think are too
difficult but we
discover what we
can do and build
and overcome and
think beyond our
little corners if
we let Him help

God asks only
what we can do
only what is right
only what will
make us better
wiser people
if we answer
"Ready!"

Genesis 25:27-34
FOOLISHNESS

How easily we
give up what
we should
love
need
cherish

Isaac and Rebekah
had twins
Esau and Jacob

Esau
traded his birthright
to his younger brother
for stew

lentil
stew
and bread
did I forget
to mention
the bread?

Genesis 28:10-16

STONY START

Jacob
chose a stone as a pillow
for that's all he could find

Perhaps
he turned this way and that
trying to get comfortable
After all,
how comfy can a rock
really be?

But
he accepted it

And when
he accepted it
he fell asleep
and dreamed
a dream of the Lord
and heaven's stairway

He awoke and knew—
the Lord was with him!

The Lord
had been with him
when he accepted the stone
when he thought himself alone
when he had nowhere to lay his head
when he had only sharp rocks in his bed

When we have nothing but a stone
to call our own, the Lord says
"I'm here."

Genesis 29:9-30
JACOB'S LOVE

Jacob loved Rachel

From the start
she won his heart
For seven years
with toil and tears
he worked the land
to win her hand

Jacob married Leah

He was tricked
He was ticked
So seven more
did he endure
Worked the land
for Rachel's hand

Jacob married Rachel

No doubt Jacob was furious
Labon's reasons? Spurious
But he did what he had to do
His love was pure and true
Jacob looked upon her face
Bore his chore with grit and grace

Can you grasp
that kind of love?
Now grasp this …

God loves you
even more than
Jacob loved Rachel

Genesis 37 and 39-46; 47:1-12

HARD TIMES

Joseph
was thrown
into a cistern
by his brothers, sold
Reported killed
to his father

Joseph
became servant
of an Egyptian
Was falsely accused
of trying to sleep
with the Egyptian's wife

Was jailed

Have you ever been
shoved down a dry well
by your own family
Sold and declared dead

Have you ever been
a slave

Have you ever
resisted temptation
remained righteous—
Locked away anyway

Would you lose
your faith
after all that

Don't think of it
as just a story
Put yourself
in Joseph's place

Your dad sends you
to find your brothers
It takes a while
but there they are
You smile
They grab you
scratch you
snatch the cloak
your dad gave you
yell, insult, lift you
throw you
somewhere
dark and dank and scary
"Come back!" you cry
but only an echo answers

Try to stop the blood
Try to stay warm
for endless hours
Try not to replay
what has happened

Finally someone comes
and you think it must
have been a horrible joke

But it is not your brothers
They are strangers
They yank you out
They do not care about
skin they scrape off your
body as they drag you
They do not care if you
pass out from the pain

They carry you away
from your home
You cannot get back
You have no power
to free yourself

28

You have no way
to let anyone know
where you are
You must do
everything you are told

So you do
everything you are told
Then the spouse
of your master
tries to seduce you
You run
Spouse lies
Situation worsens
You could easily go mad
in prison
You could easily blame
everyone, including
God

But you do not

You help others
with their dreams

They forget you

After two long years
word reaches the pharaoh
You help him
with his dreams …

And we are back
to Joseph

Pharaoh was pleased
and Joseph was given
privileges and marriage
and children and wealth
at age thirty

He had gone
to find his brothers
at age seventeen
Such a long time
to lose your life
Such a long time
to build bitterness

What would you do?

Joseph thanked God
Forgave his brothers
Reunited with family
Was generous with
food and land and love

Someone has
abandoned you
lied about you
imprisoned you
forgotten you
And you have every right
to be bitter, angry, hurt

But what if you replace a grudge
with love

Ask God to bless those you
cannot forgive
Ask God for help as Joseph did

I know, but try

Exodus 1-20

GOD'S WILL

What an odd life Moses had

Commanded by the pharaoh
to be murdered
(Hebrew male)
Hidden by his mother
(protection)
Watched by his sister
(drifting)
Rescued by the pharaoh's daughter
(pity)
Nursed by his own mother
(God's intervention)
Adopted by the pharaoh's daughter
(amazing)

Not to mention
defending a fellow Hebrew
fleeing for his life
marrying in a strange land
investigating a burning bush
conversing with God
negotiating with the pharaoh
delivering ten plagues
freeing the Israelites
parting the sea
wandering the desert
receiving ten commandments

And other ordinary stuff

Exodus 20:1-17
THE TEN COMMANDMENTS

Do we try to live by
God's rules?
Do we use the tools
He provides?

You shall not have other gods besides me.
Do you put God
before your spouse
before your children
before yourself?
Acknowledge God as the one true God
Think of Him before making decisions
All else will work out as it should
All else will work out for the good
Believe

You shall not carve idols …
You shall not bow down before them or worship them.
That
is an easy one
you say
But is it?
Do you worship God only?
Ever worshipped
a person?
a job?
money?
Praise only
God
Let only
God
lead you

You shall not take the name of the Lord, your God, in vain.
God
is not
an expression

particularly not
an expression
of anger
Your words are
a reflection
of your faith
Choose them
with care

Keep holy the sabbath day.
Things have changed
On Sunday people
work at jobs
work in the yard
work around the house
catch up on errands
go to birthday parties
attend sporting events
buy the week's groceries
move mechanically
Balance is the key
Take time for yourself
Take time for your family
Above all
Take time for God

Honor your father and your mother.
It is quite possible
that your parents
are not
perfect
Respect them
anyway
Do not yell
or talk back
Do a task asked
without grumbling
Offer
without being asked

And if your parents do
things that might make
God sad
Do not do
what they do
But be respectful

You shall not kill.
God is the only
one Who decides
when it is time
for our bodies
to die
No one
No one
No one
else
decides that

You shall not commit adultery.
So many lives
are ruined
when this commandment
is broken
When you love someone
When you marry someone
You protect that someone
Be faithful

You shall not steal.
You are not entitled
to anything
no matter how much
anyone else
has
Your money struggles
may be harder
than another person's

But every person
has
a cross to bear
You have no right
to lessen your burden
by adding to another's
And before those of you
with
money
clothes
shelter
employment
get too smug
It is your job
to reach out
to those
who have
not
And one more thing
"You shall not steal"
also means
you do not take
dreams
confidence
happiness
away
from anyone

You shall not bear false witness.
You say something
to make yourself
look better
Or someone is blamed
for your mistake
and you say nothing
Or no one saw
what you did
so you do not
speak out

Or you overhear
something not true
about someone
and do not stand up
Lies
tear
our world apart

You shall not covet.
We have been given
different births
different families
different gifts
different lives
Each is unique
Each is worth
giving thanks
to God
See what you have
Be who you are
Free yourself
from greed

Exodus 32:1-14

THE GOLDEN CALF

God rescues?
Praise Him
Memories fade?
Turn to sin

God heals?
Praise Him
Feel better?
Turn to sin

God gives?
Praise Him
Have enough?
Turn to sin

God wants us
Free from sin
God loves us
Turn to Him

It's all He wants
It's all He needs
Remember God
And believe

Not much has changed
In this present day
Like the Israelites
We turn away

A golden calf
New job, wealth
Return to safety
Restored health

They forgot
As do we
God is the one
Who sets us free

Praise God
Then forget
Is that how
Our debt is met?

Exodus 35:4-35

MATERIALS AND TALENTS

The people were asked to look into their hearts
and give what they could, silver and gold,
bronze, linens, oils, spices, precious gems ...
All could have made them wealthy if sold

But they gave
to the Lord

The people were asked to look into their hearts
and give what they could, talents and skills,
experts at embroidery, carpentry, weaving ...
All could have earned them money if willed

But they worked
for the Lord

We are asked to look into our hearts
and give what we can, money and time
a dollar here, some comfort there
helping with an hour, a dime

Can we give
to the Lord?

We are asked to look into our hearts
and give what we can, what we do best
whatever it is that we know how to do
all we love doing without any rest

Can we work
for the Lord?

Leviticus 25:1-7

LET THE EARTH REST

Chop down, burn ground
Leak oil, poison soil
Dump trash, need cash

Left to rot, parking lot
Chop down, burn ground
Leak oil, poison soil
Dump trash, need cash

Sea spills, landfills
Left to rot, parking lot
Chop down, burn ground
Leak oil, poison soil
Dump trash, need cash

Pollution, retribution

Waste embraced
Land disgraced

What part of
Give rest to the land
Did we not understand?

Leviticus 25:8-43

JUBILEE

Tenants of our Father
we do not own a thing

When someone is in trouble
and needs to sell property
We are not to charge interest
and must let them buy it back

When someone is in trouble
and needs to sell his services
We are to hire, not treat as slaves
are to be gracious, not condescending

Every fiftieth year—
this is truly the marvelous part—
All people are to return home
without fear of perpetual poverty

The cycle is broken
God has spoken

Are we listening?

Numbers 22:22-35

THE INNOCENT

Do not take out your frustration on someone, something
    innocent, loyal
Someone, something, having done nothing ever but protect you
    listen, toil

Or you may find that you are suddenly and embarrassingly
    outclassed
By an articulate, God-fearing, witty, why-did-you-do-that-to-me
    talking ass

Deuteronomy 6:4-9

THE GREAT
COMMANDMENT

Let's
imagine
giving God
the love
He gives us

If I love God
with all my heart
all my soul
all my strength
I will be
transformed

If you love God
with all your heart
all your soul
all your strength
you will be
transformed

If I love God
with all my heart
all my soul
all my strength
and you do the same
and you and you
and on and on
the world will be
transformed

Try it with me
and see
what happens

Shall we?

Deuteronomy 8:11-18
GOD GIVES

I grew this food
God gave the land

I stitched a shirt
God gave two hands

I fixed some problems
God gave a brain

I quenched my thirst
God gave the rain

I ate my fill
God gave the wheat

I ran my race
God gave fine feet

I made my money
God gave the skill

I chose this career
God gave free will

I wrote a book
God gave ability

I drew some pictures
God gave creativity

All we have and will ever be
Comes from Great Generosity

God only asks us that we learn
To kindly thank Him in return

Deuteronomy 22:1-4

CONCERN

It's so easy
to look the other way
More time-efficient
to pass by and say
"That's not my problem"

Show concern
Pay attention
to struggles
Oh, did I mention
God's request?

When an animal has
wandered or is hurt
Act with compassion
Lift it from the dirt
and send it home

If God wants us
to stop and treat
an animal kindly
should we greet
people kindly?

When a person has
wandered or is hurt
Act with compassion
Lift her from the dirt
Lead the way Home

Deuteronomy 30:1-10

MERCY

It is the Lord's delight
to bestow mercy

He does not forgive
because we are good

Our Father forgives
because He is good

Deuteronomy 30:11-14

UNDERSTANDING

You do not have to be
a spiritual leader
a brilliant thinker
a superb writer
or even a reader
to understand
God's great plan

God has not spoken it
to a select few
or hidden it
for only some
to find

God has written it
on your heart
It's something
you have always
known

When you are quiet
you feel it
When you seek God
you find Him

It's Love
It has always been there—
that tiny, tender tug

Love
God
Love
others

as God loves *you*

Deuteronomy 31:7-8

DIFFICULT TASKS

Ever been asked an impossible task—
One you should do but seems too hard for you?

When tempted you might just abandon what's right
Let God walk along. Feel God and be strong

People may leave you, displease and deceive you
Yet God walks along. Feel God and be strong

Each challenge you face can be won with God's grace
God does walk along. Feel God and be strong

Joshua 6:1-16

PERSISTENCE

Do you ever go
round and round an issue
like round and round
the wall of Jericho?
Sometimes
you just have to
keep doing what
you are doing
If you believe
your actions
are right
all will be right
in the end
and you will
blow your horn
and shout for joy

Judges 16:4-21

THINK

God gave Samson
brawn not brains
I mean, after all,
Three times
Delilah betrays him—
then Samson shares
his secret with her
and is surprised
by the attack
of the Philistines—
ummmm …
God gave us gifts
He also gave us
common sense
Use it

Ruth 1-4

DOING RIGHT

Ruth was free
to return to her family
when her husband
died

Instead
she stayed with Naomi
the mother-in-law
who needed her

She was blessed
with marriage
a home
a son

Her son Obed
became father of Jesse
who was father
of David

Yes, she was blessed
with success
for holding on tight
for doing right

We never know really
where our choices
will lead us
Do we

And yet I bet
you still try
to do what is
right

1 Samuel 3:1-11

LISTENING

Speak, Lord,
for your servant
is listening

We wish God
would speak
directly to us,
don't we?
It would make
life easier if
He would just
communicate

He does

When we have
the desire to
do something
and it works
to our advantage,
we do it, so
thank God
for the tip

When we sense
we must
do something
we do not wish to,
we go deaf and
pretend God
did not try
to converse

God speaks
to our hearts
all the time

Repeat after me ...

Speak, Lord,
for your servant
is listening

And learn to tune in

1 Samuel 3:12-13

PARENTING

It is our calling
as parents
to guide our children
as they grow
into adulthood

It is our calling
as parents
to teach our children
right ways
from wrong

It is our calling
as parents
to let our children
face consequences
for poor choices

It is our calling
as parents
to do this
for our children
gently
but to do it

If we
do not
who will?

It is our calling
as parents
to do this for
our children
because we
love them

as God loves us

1 Samuel 15:19-22

NOT SACRIFICE, BUT LOVE

Left to their own devices
the people burned sacrifices
For this was the only way they knew
to show their love for the one God true

Why do we choose
the road that leaves us bruised
the decision that proves us hollow
when all God asks is that we follow?

Can a burning
ever stop the yearning
to please God in every way?
Can we simply listen and obey?

God loves us all
To answer His call
just allow Him to hold you
Let unending Love enfold you

Let unending Love enfold you
Just allow Him to hold you
as you answer His call
For God loves us all

Can we simply listen and obey
to please God in every way?
Ever stop the yearning
with a burning?

When all God asks is that we follow
The decisions that prove us hollow
are roads that leave us bruised
Why is this what we choose?

To show their love for the one God true
this was the only way they knew
The people burned sacrifices
left to their own devices

51

1 Samuel 17:4-11, 32-51

BULLIES

There are giant Goliaths
we cannot chase away
with slingshots and stones

the way David did
But we can ask God, pray
for solutions of our own

ask for courage to tell
the bully it isn't okay—
to climb down from his throne

pray for the strength
to walk toward the day
we welcome him Home

2 Samuel 6:14-15

DAVID DANCES

Leap, twirl, skip, hop!
Show your joy nonstop!

Love the Artist?
Here's your chance!
Love the Artist?
Sing and dance!

Leap, twirl, skip, hop!
Show your joy nonstop!

2 Samuel 19:1
GRIEF

Pain in
losing
a child
is not
describable
Give your grief
to our Father
Begin to heal by
showing love to
every child
and
Remember
you are His
child, too
Let our Father
comfort you

1 Kings 3:7-12, 16-28
SOLOMON

We have heard
of Solomon's wisdom
applied to the women
who each claimed
a child as hers
of how he
gained fame
for the way he
decided the case
But do you realize
how it all began?
It began
with a prayer

1 Kings 8:39

ONLY GOD

Quick
to pick
on others

we name
their shame,
their sin

ignoring,
storing
ours

Perfect,
we neglect
our wrongs

draw attention
to dissension
of others

Hello?
Do we know
their hearts?

Hearts are lonely
Only, *only*
God

knows
what goes
on in there

1 Kings 17:7-16

HELP

You have
nothing
Just enough
to feed you,
your family
for a day
A stranger
appears
and wants
to be fed!
Is he out
of his mind?

But
you are kind,
take pity
on him,
feed him
You do not die
Your family
does not die
You could not
have predicted
this
But God did

Follow your
heart
even when
you are
desperate
Maybe—
especially
perhaps when
you are
desperate—
God knows
what to do

1 Kings 18:25-29

WHERE DOES YOUR PRAYER GO?

When you pray each day
is it to the
    God of all or god of mall
    God of mission or god of ambition
    God of time or god of crime
    God of kindness or god of blindness
    God of knowing or god of wealth growing

God listens to you
      that is, if you are praying to the Artist
        praying to God who created
        us and everything around us
Why won't the gods
      of money and power and fame answer?
        Could it be that they do not exist?
        Now we're getting somewhere

1 Kings 19:11-12

WHISPERS

We expect
God to appear
to us in
STRONG
POWERFUL
TERRIFYING
ways
We wait for
LOUD
HUGE
OBVIOUS
signs

But God
is no ruffian
He whispers
to us
He calls
to us
in tranquil
ways
He gives
subtle signs
to the meek
of heart

God
is the breeze
that touches
a cheek
God
is the silence
that stirs
a part
of us
God
is our
answer

2 Kings 2:9-11

TRAVELING TO HEAVEN

How do you think
we'll get there?
A flaming
chariot, like Elijah?
Maybe it's up to each …
An old steam locomotive
if you love landscapes
A rocket if you have
always wanted to
be an astronaut
A slow boat
rolling on the waves
A beam of light
A shooting star
A gust of wind
Maybe we'll walk
Run
Fly
All I know is I
will enjoy every
moment of the
journey in eager
anticipation
of the destination

1 Chronicles 1-9

DESCENDANTS

Wow!

Can you
even trace
your roots
back to your
great-great
grandparents?

Have you seen
the genealogy
in Chronicles?
It's inspiring

Keep a list
of your family
and pass it on
to your children
to pass on
to their children

Wow!

2 Chronicles 6:10, 32-33

WELCOME

When this masterpiece,
this dwelling house of God
was finished,
Solomon prayed
Solomon prayed
that all would be welcome
not only "his" people
but *all*
Everyone was welcome
in this masterpiece,
this dwelling house of God

Ezra 2
COUNT!

Count and count
and count again!
There is a glitch ...
Count only men!

Only the men
have real skill.
Forget women—
That's the drill.

How do I know?
I have my sources,
But you may count
mules and horses.

Forget the women,
But count the asses,
camels and gold,
silver and sashes.

Women are vital—
a finding since then!
But in Ezra's time?
Beasts and men.

Nehemiah 5
UNSELFISH

Nehemiah
was wise
a respected
governor
And yet
he took
no pay
and worked
alongside
the people
and fed them
at his
personal expense
fiercely defended
their honor
their right to be
treated fairly

We need
leaders
like that

Tobit 12[†]

CHILDREN
AND ANGELS

We don't see
the angels walking among us,
do we?
Treat all as angels of the Lord
Treat all as children of God
Be kind, be generous, and the Artist
will paint for you a beautiful life

Judith 7:19-32; 8:1-17[†]

TIMELINE

We can't give God
a timeline
a date by which He
gives us what we want
Judith, a widow with
respect for our Father,
reminded the elders
not to test our Lord

We all need reminding …
No timeline
Instead
a prayer for patience
a prayer for strength
a prayer for God's help
to handle whatever
comes our way

Esther A: 1-11; 2:1-23;
3:1-11; 4:1-16; C: 1-11;
7:9-10; 8:3-8; F: 1-6

DREAMS

Mordecai dreamed—
more of a nightmare
than a dream—
He did not understand it
and could have worried
his life away puzzling it out
But that was not his habit

Mordecai
thought about it

But in the meantime he …

Raised an orphaned cousin
as his daughter
Observed what went on
all around him
Sent Esther, the orphan,
to win the king's favor
Saved the king
from an evil plot
Refused to bow down
to anyone but God
Learned of a decree
to kill his Jewish people
Asked Esther to intervene
and speak to the king
Prayed to God for aid
Fasted on Esther's behalf

In the end Mordecai saw
what the dream meant and
how God had saved them

If he had worried
his life away, puzzling it out
instead of continuing to do what he
believed right in God's sight
the ending may have been
quite different, quite sad

Contemplate dreams
Examine thoughts
But keep in mind
that you ought
to take action, too

1 Maccabees 1:41-63; 2 Maccabees 7†

STAND FOR GOD

You may be persecuted
    for your faith in God, your belief in love
Chances are you may hear unkind words
But most likely you'll never experience the horrendous acts
    that others have suffered as they stood for God
Do not give in to evil
Stand for God
At the same time
    do not harm others
    who practice their love for God in different ways
Different does not mean wrong
Love God
Be tolerant
Show kindness
If you stand for God
    you stand for Love and Peace
You stand for something greater than our limited selves

2 Maccabees 6:12-13[†]

REBUKE

We grumble, grunt, gripe
When we experience a
Natural consequence
For a wrong action
Relax …
That is God

Our Father wants to help us
Wants us to slow down
Think about what we
Are doing before
We get in
Over our heads

Job
SUFFERING

Oh, Job!

Job
had everything
Job gave thanks
to God

But
suddenly
His herds
were gone
His children
were dead
He tore his clothes
yet did not speak
against God

Job was covered
in sores
His wife
begged him to
speak against God
yet he did not

His friends
urged him to
ask God
for forgiveness
for surely
he must have done
something wicked
but Job knew
he had not sinned
It was not God's
punishment

Everything horrible
that could come
to one person
came to Job
Still
in the end
Job believed
in God's ultimate
Love, unlimited
Wisdom

Go, Job!

Psalm 4:9
REST

I toss, turn at night
   restless with worry
   trying to hurry
   the first morning light

Would it not be sweet
   if I could let go
   if I could just know
   God sleeps at my feet?

Psalm 13
GOD ANSWERS

Feel forgotten, lonely
Thinking, *If only*
God were here…?

Ever wonder why
God lets you cry
Deserts you?

God answers prayer
God is there
sheltering you

God will see you
through
Be patient

Psalm 22:1-19

HOW DID THEY KNOW?
PART ONE

How did they know
So long ago
What Christ would undergo?

Impaled hands
Harsh commands
Tunic taken
Then forsaken
Parched throat
Crowd gloats
He's mocked
Bones knocked
Fastened feet
Life complete

Consigned since conception
Resigned
To cruel reception

(continued at Zechariah 9:9-10)

Psalm 23
COMFORT

What comfort
Psalm 23
can be

What absence
of fear
when God is near

What guidance
God gives
so we may live

What future
we're able
to have at God's table

What peace
to know
God loves us so

Psalm 28:7

THANKSGIVING

when we think
Thanksgiving
do we think
gravy, potatoes, turkey
rich cranberry sauce
cookies and pies
stomachs too full
to move

or

do we think
giving thanks
to
God

thank God
thank God for food
thank God for work
thank God for family
thank God for friends
thank God for purpose
thank God for miracles
thank God for life

Psalm 78
ALLEGIANCE

God helps us
We turn away
God helps us
We turn away
God helps us
We turn away

See a pattern?

Maybe it's time
We say thank You
and turn around

Psalm 100
JOY

Sing! Sing!
Sing on high!
Sing! Sing!
    God is nigh!
Sing! Sing!
Sing along!
Sing! Sing!
    Sing God's song!

Psalm 104
ALL

All are part of Your great plan
From microscopic to great sky
You shape all beasts and every man
Hear each whisper, feel each sigh

I can never understand
Your ways or how You do these things
The brush, the touch of Your soft hand
Goodness that You always bring

Psalm 106
SIN

Admit you have a problem
Isn't that what they say—
those One-Day-at-a-
Time programs?

Those programs
do not expect
us to get
it all at once

That is why
they make
us take
baby steps

That is why
as we stumble
we tumble
into His arms

Psalm 118:24
THIS DAY

complain, mumble
grieve and grumble
forget my blessings
tired, transgressing
name every wrong
blame all day long
fail and regret
somehow forget …

I am a child of God

Have you forgotten, too?
Guess what we should do …

Rejoice! Show love!
Praise Artist above!
Find a way to rewind!
Start over! Be kind!

We are children of God!

Psalm 131
HUMILITY

Whatever you do, grand or small
Hold God's wondrous plan in awe

Still your soul, quiet your mind
Leave all smugness well behind

Whatever you do, remain observant
Hold yourself as His humble servant

Psalm 139:1-14

ALL KNOWING,
ALWAYS WITH US

Our Father
Holds us
        before we're born
Soothes us
        before each morn
Guides us
        with each step
Fills us
        with each breath
Hugs us
        when we fall
Hears us
        when we call
Lives in us
        with each kind deed
Gives to us
        with all we need
Meets us
        in joys and sorrows
Leads us
        in new tomorrows

Our Father
Knows us
Is with us
Loves us

Proverbs 1:4-5

PURPOSEFUL PROVERBS

Do you think
the Bible
too hard?

The Book
of Proverbs
promises
that even
the young
will learn

Do you think
the Bible
not enough?

The Book
of Proverbs
promises
that even
the wise
will learn

Neat trick,
huh?
There is
something
in there
for everyone

Proverbs 1:8-19
WHICH WAY?

Come along! Come along!
How carefree the way of the wicked
How easy for them to get rich
     at the expense
         of the innocent

This way! This way!
How enticing their words to the ear
How easy for them to kill
     for the wealth
         of the innocent

Come along! Come along!
How rocky the way of the honest
How dusty the path one follows
     at no expense
         of the innocent

This way! This way!
How great the words of our Father
How proud He is of His children
     for the wealth
         of the innocent heart

Proverbs 3:28
ATTITUDE

Your neighbor
needs you now
not tomorrow

Time is
not for you
to borrow

Proverbs 5:15-20
ADULTERY

Clear
pure
water
from
your
own
flowing
fountain

That's the most refreshing
That's your source of joy
That's the place you go
For love, acceptance, tenderness
Why would you want to splash anywhere else?

Proverbs 8
FOR THE WISE

Wisdom is
  true
    honest
      noble
        knowledgeable
          sincere
            experienced
              strong
                understanding
              just
                dutiful
  and
with God when He created the universe

I want the teacher Wisdom please
Would anyone like to join me?

Proverbs 9:7-9
FOR THE ARROGANT

When you do not like what I have to say
I rudely ask you to be on your way
If you disagree with my perfect view
My response is to ask, "And who are you?"
Challenge my motives, I'll tell you to pack
I have the brilliance that all others lack

Just look at that person standing there
Smiling and acting as if she might care
As if a correction could help her learn
As if other voices should have a turn
Why isn't she curt, why doesn't she cry
And why is that person smarter than I?

Proverbs 10:19
CONTROL

We like to hear ourselves speak
listen to the sound of our voices
pay no attention to the
worth of our words
as long as we
are heard

Instead of talking for the echo
let's pray first and offer
wise words when we can
and when we cannot
let's be quiet
okay?

Proverbs 11:29

OUR HOUSEHOLD

why do we upset
those who mean the most to us?
cherish, *cherish* them

Proverbs 12:18

WORDS OF KINDNESS

Whisper healing
with true feeling

From your lips
let nothing slip
but words of kindness

Proverbs 14:31

ALMS GIVING

Are you
Looking to
Make the Artist
Smile?

Give to those
In need
Victory!
Instantly, God
Nods and
Grins

Proverbs 15:17

A SERVING
OF LOVE

Simple sustenance
shared with family
breaking bread
laughter, stories

or

Extravagant dishes
table set with malice
tasting bitterness
tears, harsh words

Which?

Proverbs 16:31
GROWING OLD

It's hard growing older
We miss our youth
our energy, our strength
We miss our smooth skin
shiny hair, thin waists
We want our carefree lives
with no mortgages, no debt
We want to stay out late
and sleep in, wake up rested

But we have learned so much
We have grown as people
obtained wisdom in God's eyes
We have fought battles
and stood up for what's right
We accept that what's been gained
far outweighs the cost
We know that God is pleased
when we bow our gray heads

Proverbs 17:14
BREATHE

On edge
        I am right on the edge
I can taste the tension
        Feel my frustration
I do not like what you are saying
        Do not like it at all
You should agree with me
        Tell me I am right

I am right on the edge
        On edge
I am not listening to you
        Cannot hear you
Waiting for my turn to talk
        To make my point
You should tell me I am right
        Agree with me

Unless
        Breathe
Unless I let myself hear you
        Breathe
Unless I meet you halfway
        Breathe
Unless I realize this is trivial
it will lead to a fight

Let me look at you
   my child
     my neighbor
       the one I love
         my friend in need
           another human being like me

I choose to breathe and look at you
through God's eyes—eyes of compassion
I don't remember why I was mad

Proverbs 18:11-12
ME!

Me! Me, me, me!
Look at what I've done!
My effort is weightless!
See! See, see, see!
Look at what I've won!
Admire my greatness!

You're leaving me?
I lack humility?
Okay, I'll try it …
But can I buy it?

Proverbs 21:6
A LIE

A lie …
bright balloon on cacti

Proverbs 21:14

HELPING SECRETLY

Ever given
in secret
to alleviate
a debt?
Or better yet
just to bring
someone
a smile?
Give it a go
It will be
worthwhile

Proverbs 22:6

LITTLE ONES

What do we teach our little ones, little ones
    What do we teach them each day?
When we teach them love and respect for God
    We teach them not to stray

Why do we teach our little ones, little ones
    Why do we teach what is right?
When we teach them truth and honor and grace
    We teach it's faith, not sight

Proverbs 23:4-5

WEALTH

Nothing is certain
in this life
We can work
and save
and strive
to build
for retirement
or our child's
education
or security
or peace
of mind
And
in an instant
it can disappear
Instead
work
and save
and strive
to build
life everlasting
by trusting
the Artist

His Love
is a sure bet

Proverbs 24:17-18

ENEMIES

Human tendency is to say *HA*
when enemies crumble, crash

We are better than that
We are made in God's image

Pray for enemies who meet disgrace
Pray for them to turn to God

We are all
in this together

Proverbs 31:10-11

SPOUSE

Be good to your spouse
Let that person know
His or her worth

Be good to your spouse
Let that person know
You appreciate her or him

Be good to your spouse
Let that person know
That in him or her

You
See
God

Ecclesiastes 3:1-8

A TIME FOR
EVERYTHING

The author of
Ecclesiastes
felt all was
vanity

and yet

he gives
us such
beautiful
verses

A time for
everything

Sometimes
we must
wait, must
slow down
until the right
time to act

Sometimes
we will
be happy

but that will not last

Sometimes
we will
be unhappy

but that, too, will pass

Understand
that we change
that the world changes

and yet

We experience
the same thing

We all live
We all die
It's what we choose to do
with the time between
that matters

Song of Songs 2:8-14

A LOVE SONG

Who would not want
A love song
A poem
Something that says you are

Beautiful, loved, wanted
needed, cherished, adored
You are the light
in your lover's eyes!

He beckons you
Whispers his love
Longs to hold you
close to his heart

Every sorrow
has passed
Every tomorrow
you will share

That kind of love
is hidden on earth
We may love and marry
and care for others

But that deep, true, eternal
Love that outlasts all?
That sweet, strong song ...
that voice calling you?

That is God
loving *you*
unconditionally
for all time

Wisdom 4:7-14[†]

EARLY DEATH

"Only the good die young"
Is there something to that
song? I don't know
I do know that while it is

beyond our comprehension
whatever the person's age
death brings us into the
presence of God

We suffer the loss here—
But the person who dies?
God is holding that sweet,
sweet child and all is well

Sirach 11:3†

CHOICE

A vulture spreads its massive wings
one thousand feet above the ground
It searches for decaying things
triumphant when the flesh is found

Strong sense of smell, keen steady eyes
with beak that crushes to tear meat
The vulture homes in on the cries
that lead it to the wasting weak

Bee does no harm but extricates
the rich deep juice for honey's treat
Helps beauty spread, to procreate
with dust of pollen on its feet

If vulture's strength were offered me
no mercy, death to all who live
I'd choose the simple drone of bee
to inhale fragrance and forgive

Isaiah 1:18

RETURN

Have you ever felt so dirty
You thought you'd never be clean?
Have you ever done something awful
Then hoped you had not been seen?

God was with you. He saw you sin.
But that doesn't stop Him loving you so.
Seek truth. Pray. Listen. Change your way.
Let God wash you "white as snow."

Isaiah 2:2-5
ZION

The images …
"swords into plowshares"
"spears into pruning hooks"
… images of weapons
turned into tools
to help, not harm

The images …
"nor shall they train for war"
"let us walk in the light"
… images of glorious days
spent in peace, tranquility
climbing as one to Zion

Isaiah 6:5-8
WHOM SHALL I SEND?

Do you feel unworthy
to answer God's call?
A great prophet
felt just like that
Angels assured Isaiah
that he could do it

We can do
anything
everything
God asks
if we reply
"Here I am!"

Isaiah 7:14; 9:5-6; 11:1-10

PROPHECY IN THE EIGHTH CENTURY B.C.

A virgin has a child?
Do not be ridiculous
A peaceful dominion
in this time of war?
What do you mean by
walking in darkness?
What light?
Who judges the poor justly?
A lion sharing the food of an ox?
Now you are making me hoot!
And ... and, oh ... my belly hurts
from laughing so hard—
All this is to be accomplished
by the coming of a CHILD?
I am roaring!
Ah, hmmm ... thanks for the laugh
Isaiah, where *do* you get your info?

Isaiah 31:6-7

WHOSE HANDS?

Turn not to
what you have molded
with your two hands
Turn to
the Artist who shaped
you with His love

Isaiah 40:3

PREPARE!

Centuries later
John did cry out
to prepare the
way of our Lord

Do you prepare
a path for Him
Do you pull the
weeds of sin

Do you sweep it
free of evil thoughts
Do you keep clear
a path to your soul

Isaiah 43:23-25

FORGETTING

Of course God knows when we gripe and complain
Of course God knows when we try to explain
God sees the times when we put ourselves first
God sees the times when we quench our own thirst

but

God forgets the times when we break His laws
God forgets the trouble His children cause
We cannot make God forget, nor deceive
God chooses to do so, never to leave

Isaiah 49:14-16
YOUR NAME

Hush, my sweet child,
do not cry
I, your Lord,
am lullaby

Etched on my palm
is your name
With me, child,
you shall remain

Like parents soothe
a child at night
I, your Lord,
will hold you tight

Isaiah 53:4-7
FOR US

Glimpse the suffering
God took from us by giving
His one Son for us

Isaiah 54:11-12

STORM-BATTERED

Alone?
Never!
You
are
God's
darling
own

Isaiah 55:8-11

HIS WORD AS SEED

Our thoughts can be scattered
—even scatter-brained
God's thoughts are not man's
—not for us to understand

God scatters his Word
—with a higher purpose
He sends it out to nourish
—it returns with a flourish

Isaiah 58:6-7

WHAT GOD ASKS

God does not ask us for food fasting
He asks that we do something lasting
for others

What does it matter if you skip a meal
but then choose not to deal
with others?

Give your time instead
Give your kindness and bread
to others

Isaiah 58:9

AWESOME REVERSE

Go to Isaiah 58:9
Read that line

Back to Isaiah 6:8
Contemplate

Make the connection
It's time for reflection

Jeremiah 13:1-11

LOOK

If we look around
we are bound
to learn something
about God, about us
He reveals Truth in the
everyday, in the
cause-and-effect,
common-sense stuff we
see but do not notice
If we hide our faith
beneath a rock, never
use it, never
wear it in public,
afraid to openly
show our love for God,
our faith will rot
Our faith is not
designed to be showy
but it *is* designed
to be practical, to be
purposeful, an active part
of our lives, not
buried in dark crevices
of cold, stone hearts

Jeremiah 20:7-9
HONEST PETITION

When you pray
      is it formal?
Instead of
      "You are holy"
Jeremiah said
      "You tricked me!"

God does not desire
      formality
God desires
      honesty

If you feel elated, sedated, frightened, enlightened,
      energized, pulverized
Say something
      God knows your heart
      as God knew Jeremiah's
      He will not be surprised
      God welcomes you—
      joy, doubts, and all

In the same way
      When you thirst
      feel like you will burst
      unless you speak of God

Say something
      like Jeremiah

Jeremiah 22:3

REMINDER FOR REMAINDER OF DAYS

The Artist reminds us
time and again that
our lives will be
works of art
if we do what is right
Be fair. A splash of color!
Protect the innocent. A perfect stroke!
Be kind to visitors, to those who are alone.
       The finishing touch!
Is it asking too much
to do what is right
in exchange for becoming
a work of art?

Jeremiah 23:25-32

FALSE PROPHETS

are

Depriving
Innocent
Recipients of
Truth

You grasp in your heart that it is a lie
when you hear a self-server prophesy

Jeremiah 46:28
WE ARE HIS

You will not abandon your children
Our Father will not abandon us

You would not let your children
do something wrong without speaking
to them or making sure they learn
a lesson in a firm but gentle way
whether it is having your children
repair something they have damaged
expecting they help someone they hurt
requiring an apology when needed
explaining why something was wrong
preparing them to make better choices
suggesting they pray when they stray

Our Father does that for us, too
How could He not?

Lamentations 5:14-21
LEAD US BACK

Up
pull you
God will
Ask and
your neglect
Reflect upon
the bottom?
been at
you ever
Have

Baruch 4:28†

AS MANY TIMES

We tell our toddlers no
and take the time to show
as many times as it takes
for them to understand wrong

We teach them what is right
and express our delight
as many times as it takes
for them to internalize good

God knows it may take a lifetime
of *No*s and *Right*s for us to
understand wrong
internalize good

God will tutor us
as many times as it takes

Ezekiel 3:3-4

NOURISHMENT

I like spinach pizza
with a glass of red wine
Chocolate and peanut butter?
Mmmm … they're sublime

I'll bet that you, too
have your favorite foods
delectable dishes
that lead to good moods

Have you tried filling up
on the most satisfying?
Dine on God's Word—
No calories. I'm buying

Ezekiel 12:7
LET GOD

We carry our burden into darkness
    knowing
That though we do not see the end of the
    road
God will take us where we need to
    be
He will relieve us of our heavy
    load
And from our worries set us
    free
It's okay to let God do the
    towing

Ezekiel 16:1-16, 59-63
SHAME

How easy to forget
the good God does
How incensed we get
when He takes from us
to make us think
about our actions

Spoiled children

Ezekiel 33:11
WAITING

God is heartbroken
when we die guilty
do not face our sin
do not return to Him

God is never happier
than when we walk
through His front door
lost no more

Ezekiel 47:7-12
WONDERFUL WATER

Imagine
  a refreshing river
  filled with life
  lined with trees
  trees that give food
  with their fruit
  and medicine
  with their leaves

  This flowing water
  is a return to the
  paradise we left
  paradise we will have again
  with the Artist who designed it
  the Gardener who cultivated it
  the Gardening Artist who wants to share it
Imagine

Daniel 3:4-24, 90-95

FACING FIRE

Your enemy breaks into your home while you and your friends
are chatting about the weather, about your family
about how good God is
The day is hot yet the enemy forces you
to put on coats and hats and shoes
then ties you up, lights your house on fire
leaves you and your friends to burn

Now, what if you did this voluntarily?
Someone asks you to worship a golden statue
You say you only worship the one true God
Your enemy says he will throw you into a furnace
You refuse to bow to the statue
You say God can save you, but acknowledge that
for His own reasons, He might not

Either way, you would rather die than turn from your Creator
That is the real power here

God sent His angel Azariah to protect the three
thrown into the furnace, wearing coats and hats and shoes
God is loving and can do anything
so the marvelous things God accomplishes
should not surprise us

But people standing up for God?
That surprises us. The faith. The strength.

Maybe one day it will not be so shocking
when a person shows that much love for God
Maybe one day we will stand up to the bullies
the tormentors, the oppressors, the tyrants
and say, *Do your worst, for God is with us*
He will save us now or welcome us into His holy kingdom

Either way, we are no longer afraid of you
We put our trust in God alone
and invite you, like Nebuchadnezzar, to do the same

Daniel 6:1-24

THE LIONS' DEN

You have been cast
into the lions' den,
haven't you?

We all have.

Someone we thought
was a friend
betrays us.

A group
excludes us
out of jealousy.

Our earned promotion
goes to
the boss's niece.

We feel
vulnerable,
attacked.

Isn't anyone on our side?

When you
are thrown
to the lions …

Have faith.

Trust that God
will send someone
to free you.

No person or group or boss
can destroy your faith
unless you let them.

Hosea 3
WAIT FOR ME

Patience
Patience

Waiting for a loved one
Waiting for our God

Patience to wait for
forgiveness

And He will love us
And He will take us back

And we shall truly be
"Children of the living God"

Joel 1:3
PASS IT ON!

What do you tell your children?
Is religion too private for your children?
Is God too personal for your children?

If you do not discuss these things
your children will never grow
in faith

Share prayer with your children
Talk faith with your children
Feel God's glow with your children

Be an example
of His Love

Amos 4:1-3

CONSEQUENCES

God protects those who are weak
Do you think He will not speak
   on their behalf?
God mourns for those who are slain
Do you think He will abstain
   from justice?

God sees when you swindle those in need
Do you think that your greed
   will be ignored?
The day of judgment is coming
It is a slow train humming
   along the tracks
You will atone for all things cruel
You will be the mule,
   a load on your back

Now pray for insight
   to do what is right
   before the Light
   of the iron horse
   illuminates sins
   and roars past
   leaving the mules
   to trudge along
   carrying crime
   in rotting slime

Obadiah 1:17

HOPE

Hope is given
Over and over that we might not
Perish because, despite our sins, God loves us for
Eternity

Jonah 1-4
JONAH AND THE FISH

Such a short book in the Bible
that you are liable
   to miss it, to skip it
   but you'd miss one heck
   of a story, sailors on deck
   of a ship with a grip
   on Jonah—maker of this mess
They cried to the Lord in distress
   but did as bid to calm the sea
   when Jonah said, "Get rid of *me*"
God told Jonah what to say
   to Nineveh ... He ran away!
Now Jonah's only desperate wish
   was to leave the belly of this fish
Three days pleading fitfully passed
   when God answered Jonah's prayer at last
The fish spat Jonah upon the sand
   so he could follow the Lord's command
Jonah knew Nineveh would be destroyed,
   its earthly riches no longer enjoyed
The people repented with humble shame
The Lord relented, removed their blame
Jonah grew angry ... Again ran away!
He'd said what the Lord had told him to say—
Yet nothing happened. Nineveh stood,
   one hundred twenty thousand in neighborhoods
Jonah never understood his part
   in helping to turn Nineveh's hearts
His stubbornness, his pumped-up pride
   hardened his heart, led him to hide
I sometimes, too, ignore God's grace,
   let anxiety take faith's place
I'll try to learn from Jonah's tale,
   free myself from crushing whale
When the Lord gives me a task to do
   I'll pray for strength to see it through

Micah 7:5-7
TRUST

For the most part I believe
fellow beings
are good
We must, though, beware
People are, well … people …
humans with human frailties
Man cannot be and should not be
perfect
They will fail us
Willingly or reluctantly or ignorantly
They will fail us
And we will fail them

In God only must we trust

Don't give up on family, friends
They do their best, after all
We do our best, after all
We must, though, be alert
We are in the end … people …
humans with human vanities
Man can be and should be
seeking Truth. Until then
we will fail them
Easily or harshly or intelligently
we will fail them
And they will fail us

In God only must we trust

Micah 7:18-20
TRUE PROMISE

God's promise
is a true promise
No need to fret
to ask if He
really
meant it

To those who repent
our Father promises
forgiveness
Not forgivenessbutIknow
whatyoudidandIwillholda
secretgrudgeforgiveness

Real
forgiveness
where every sin is washed
away by a sea of compassion
God wants us to join Him
so He gives us every, every
chance to empty our wrongdoing
into a vast empty space
where sins disappear
and God's promise becomes
reality

Nahum 3:12

COME

We think we are so strong

Nothing can harm us
We can save ourselves
can protect our family
We surround ourselves with
sturdy walls of solid brick
　　　The trick
is to keep others out
keep our stockpile in

It's an illusion
Those are not bricks
held together with mortar
but thin limbs
quaking in wind
shaking, fledgling figs
loosening their weak grasp …
cast to ground
ground underfoot

Be strong of heart instead
　　　Tread
lightly on the feelings of others
Do not shut them out
Share not only your goods
but the good within you

Connect, confess
Bless, be blessed
as cold fortress
of clay melts away
in day's sun

And you will breathe
And you will live

You will see beauty
in every life here
You will find awe
in what is to be

You've spent enough time
in your self-made prison

Come
Walk in the Light

Habakkuk 3:17-19
FAITHFUL PRAISE

Though the world
   crumbles around us
Though mighty winds
   cease to blow
Though bodies of water
   vanish
There is one thing that
   I know

God will never abandon
God always hears our call
Upon the highest summit
God keeps us standing tall

When those around us flee
When trouble fills our days
God is still among us
We offer faithful praise

Zephaniah 1:18
DO WE GET IT?

do we understand
that money means not a thing
when God calls us home?

Haggai 1:5-6

FOR GOD,
FOR OTHERS

We store for ourselves only
and then are surprised to find
that over time
we have gained nothing

We work hard, harder
without getting ahead
In fact, we instead
lose what little we have

But what if we were to look
at our neighbors' needs,
try to control our greed?
We might discover joy!

Each kindness is a piece
of the temple He desires
We are the laborers He hires
to build a place for all

where our Lord is welcome

Zechariah 9:9-10
HOW DID THEY KNOW?
PART TWO
(continued from Psalm 22:1-19)

The Book of Zechariah
was written over 500
years before Christ
And yet it tells of
a king, a savior
humble and riding on an ass
proclaiming peace
setting prisoners of sin free
I ask again: *How did they know?*

Malachi 1:2
QUESTIONING

Our Lord loves us
Yet we question
question, question
Why?

We are loved
Let's accept that
We are loved
Let's believe that
We are loved
Let's welcome that
We are loved
Let's share that
We are loved

Let's hold that in our hearts
in our souls for now and
for all eternity
Our Lord *loves us*

Matthew 1:18-25; 2:1-23

P(R)AY ATTENTION

Your wife-to-be
is pregnant
The baby
is not yours
In a dream
an angel says
she has conceived
through the
Holy Spirit
You welcome her

Magi travel
a great distance
to bring gifts to
the newborn king
In a dream
they are warned
not to report
to Herod
They return by
another route

In a dream
you are told
to take your
wife and child
leave the country
in the night
You go and
do not move again
till told it is safe
In a dream, God speaks softly

Deep dreams
should be explored
Forceful feelings
not ignored

Matthew 3:1-12

JOHN

Prepare the way of the Lord
Strong voice crying out in the barrenness of the land
    to the barren hearts of sinners
Prepare the way of the Lord
Strong body living off nature, taking nothing from anyone,
    relying on God's Word alone
Prepare the way of the Lord
Strong faith, challenging those who mock God's plan
    by pretending they already know it
Prepare the way of the Lord
Strong humility, acknowledging that the One coming
    is far greater than he or any other

Feel that strength. Get to know it intimately.
Let it surge through your being.
Prepare the way of the Lord

Matthew 3:13-17

WORK OF ART

Picture this work of art
A river shimmering in the sun
Two men, waist-deep
Watchers scattered on the banks
Water poured slowly over one man's head
Heavens opening to this man. *Heavens opening*
The Spirit of God resting on this man. *The Spirit of God*
The voice of God speaking to this man. *The voice of God*
The message?
God is pleased. God is *pleased* with His Son
    His beloved *Son*
Frame that moment
Hang it in your mind's museum
Visit often

Matthew 4:1-11

REASONS

We are tempted
       aren't we?
We justify our actions
       don't we?
We find reasons
       I need it—God will not mind this one wrongdoing
       I deserve what others have
Even the "reason" that "the Bible says so"
We can twist passages to mean just what we want them to mean
       but …
We know what's right
       don't we?
We can stand firm
       can't we?
We can find reasons
       I didn't earn this—I am obedient to God
       I am satisfied, grateful for what I have
Even the true reason that "the Bible will lead me" if I let it
       instead of imposing a meaning
If we pray and read the Bible, God will make the message clear, no twisting

Now …
Jesus was tempted
       wasn't He?
Jesus held onto right
       didn't He?
He found reasons
       I live by God's Word—I do not test Him
       I worship God alone, not riches, not evil
And the reason? "It is written."
Jesus knew the Scriptures, as did the devil
The difference?
Jesus did not twist God's meaning for His own purposes

Let's not bend the Bible to our advantage either

Matthew 4:18-22

ANSWER HIS CALL

Would you follow if He called you?
Would you drop it all—
    your work, your way of life?
Could you do this
    from an inner, instinctive faith you did not even guess you possessed
        until He spoke your name?
After all, He was just the carpenter's son
Could you walk away
    from everything, everyone you knew
        and do so *immediately* without hesitation?

Did the first disciples ask
    Where are we going?
        What will we do?
            What will we eat?
No
They just followed

Why do we have such a hard time?

Matthew 4:23-25

HIS MINISTRY

Preaching, teaching, reaching out
Curing, assuring, removing doubt
When He spoke, people heard
He had the touch, He had the Word

Decapolis, Jerusalem, Galilee …
They came to Him to be set free
from pain, oppression, binding doubt
Preaching, teaching, reaching out

Matthew 5:1-12

SERMON ON THE MOUNT

Which is your favorite?
Do you want to be a peacemaker,
    a child of God?
Do you take courage that, sad now,
    you will find comfort?
Does it help to be told that your mercy
    will be returned to you?
Pick a favorite, but try out the others, too

Blessed are...

...the poor in spirit: Put your faith in God alone, not possessions. Live modestly. Do not cling to anything that will crumble. Be humble

...they who mourn: Be sad not only for those who lose their lives, but for those who lose their way spiritually. Pray that all may find God but let them choose the path. You cannot force faith. Lead gently, quietly. Be patient

...the meek: Understand that all you do is through the power of God. Do not pat yourself on the back and hold yourself up as better than others. Be thankful

...they who hunger and thirst for righteousness: In God's kingdom, no injustice will be done against you, against anyone. Work steadfastly toward that goal here on earth. Begin now

...the merciful: God will show you the mercy you show others. Please think before judging

...the clean of heart: Admit guilt. Try again. Prepare your heart for God. Repeat

...the peacemakers: How can we hurt one another and justify it? Wise, compassionate, knowledgeable people look for true answers to reconciliation. Be one

...they who are persecuted for the sake of righteousness: God asks that when you hear His name defiled, or see someone punished for his or her faith, that you speak up. Pray for the strength to keep standing up if it is the right thing to do

Pray. Speak. Act. See the attitudes
Be the attitudes of Christ

Matthew 5:14-16
SHINE!

Do you shine?
Do you live?
Do you give
your heart each time?

Can people tell
you're a Christian?
Is your mission
to love, love well?

Matthew 5:21-24
A GOOD HEART

On the outside
you may give
and be kind
Yet God sees
your heart
your mind

To truly love
your Father
love others
Make amends
with neighbors
with brothers

Then offer God
your *whole* heart
ready to serve
Offer no less
than what He
deserves

Matthew 5:27-32

BE TRUE

Do not look at another and daydream. Look at your husband, your wife. *That* is the person for you. God put someone on this earth for *you*. You are meant to share your experiences, your stories, your everything with that one special someone.

See your spouse. *See* your soul mate. Count your blessings! You stray the moment you envision another in your arms.

About divorce. Jesus does not want us to divorce. Once we make a commitment, we need to stick with it … "unless the marriage is unlawful." Jesus does not ask that we remain in an abusive or cheating partnership. We all deserve real love.

But Jesus does ask that we hold onto our marriage despite small inconveniences and minor differences of opinion and issues that can be solved if we only get off our lazy tushes and *work it out*. Your marriage, your partner? Worth the effort.

Matthew 5:33-37

OATHS

I swear to God!
I swear on my mother's life!
I swear on my grave!

Jesus asks
Why?

Yes means yes.
No means no.

What else is there?

Matthew 5:38-42

AND SO, CHANGE BEGINS

And so
Jesus begins
to turn
what was learned
around

Outrageous!
They, we, were taught
retaliation!

Jesus says
to let them do their worst?
to let them be our curse?

They slap one cheek?
Let them slap the other!
They take one coat?
Let them have another!

Have we learned to think
the way Jesus taught
thousands of years ago?

or is this concept still new?

Matthew 6:1-4

YOUR FATHER SEES

Do you give
    because others are watching
    because you want to look good
    because it's nice to be thanked
    because you feel pressured to do so
Examine your motives

Give
    because no one is watching
    because it makes you feel good
    because they won't know whom to thank
    because you'd like to do so
If you give only because others expect it or you will look bad if you don't
    or you feel superior when thanked or, worse, out of guilt … Stop

Your Father wants you to give freely
    with an open heart
    with a generous spirit
    with kindness
    with devotion
    with a genuine desire to help

You decide what you *want* to do
    —teach an adult to read; serve at a soup kitchen; organize a clothing drive;
    bring meals to the homebound; donate to causes in which you believe;
    give away possessions and live simply; drive cancer patients to treatment;
    crochet blankets for nursing homes; become a foster parent; reach out—

When you choose with a *willing* soul
you will have no need for anyone to see
but your Father

Matthew 6:5-15

AN INTIMATE CONVERSATION

Prayer is not for show. Prayer is an intimate
conversation between you and your Father.
Prayer is taking a walk and appreciating the
miracle of nature. Prayer is a thank-You. Prayer
is not demanding good things, but asking for the
strength to endure whatever comes your way.
Prayer is acknowledging a Power greater than
yourself. Prayer is receiving, offering forgiveness.
Prayer is humble. Prayer is kindness in action.

Matthew 6:16-18

PRIVILEGE

You've met those people, right?
The ones who work so hard, so
terribly, terribly hard, day and night?

Exhausting to serve others—their faces show it.
They fast and sacrifice and give, give, give—
making darn well certain you know it.

Offer kindness for heaven's sake, not a pat on the back.
It's not a burden to give up something or to help someone.
It's a privilege God allows. That's the perception those others lack.

Matthew 6:19-21
YOUR TREASURE

Can you carry gold when you die?
Bring money to heaven? Let's see you try.
Measure your treasure on earth.
Measure your treasure. What is *it* worth?

Fill your heart with gifts that last
Money shall be a thing of the past.
Measure your treasure on earth.
Measure your treasure. What are *you* worth?

Can you carry faith, forgiveness?
Bring love to heaven? This, God will witness!
Measure your treasure on earth.
Measure your treasure. What is *God* worth?

Matthew 6:22-23
SEEING

It's how we look at things,
isn't it?
If we look at the world
as if each person
is a brother or sister
we cannot help but try
to make the world better
for them, for us

If we look at the world
as if most people
are our enemies
then our hearts are filled
with hatred and
we cannot help but try
to destroy the world
and, in the process, destroy
them, us

Fill yourself with Light,
Goodness
by looking at the world
as Jesus did

Look through His eyes
What a view it is

Matthew 6:24

GOD OR MONEY?

God is not against money

God is against using money
for pleasure only
while others suffer
God is against making money
a priority
over family, friends, the poor
God is against money
as a symbol of power
as a way to control others
as a means to put yourself first
God is against loving money
more than loving Him

If you love God above all else
money will be used to purchase
necessities and some things
we like but more importantly
it will be used
to help others
and it will never
come before
God

When you find yourself thinking
about money and planning how
to make it and spend it and
realize those thoughts and actions
take up even a fraction of time
better spent in prayer
it is time for a change

Matthew 6:25-34

WORRY LESS, BELIEVE MORE

What if I don't make friends?
What if I don't make the team?
What if I don't fit in?

What if I don't graduate?
What if I don't find a job?
What if I don't meet my soul mate?

What if I am not a good parent?
What if my kids are unhappy?
What if I am unhappy?

Some worries are
insignificant
What if this makes me look fat?

Some worries are
deeper
What if the cancer comes back?

They all have one thing
in common
They are a waste of time

God *knows* our needs and
wants to take care of us
He *loves* us

If you do not trust God to
protect, comfort, save
Whom can you trust?

Give your worries to God
He'll hold your worries in one hand
He'll hold you with the other

Matthew 7:1-5

JUDGMENT

I judge people
I compare myself to them

How could he say that?
Why did she do that?
I am nicer than she
I am better than he
If I were that person
      I would have said this, done that
I am right
      I am in God's sight
Ooops ... yes ...
      I am in God's sight

He knows the motives of others
      I do not
He knows the motives of my heart
      I forgot
I am responsible for my words, my actions, my thoughts
I am asked to move forward on my spiritual journey
God did not say
      "Hey, give me a hand, would you?
      Do you think I should condemn that one?
      Do you think I should give that one a break?"

For heaven's sake
And I do mean *for heaven's sake*
I need to be harder on myself
Easier on others

Matthew 7:7-11

SO SIMPLE

A child sits on the front steps, crying
When Dad joins her, the child
explains that she has scraped a knee
Dad cleans it up, gets a bandage
"Why didn't you just ask?" he says

A teen sits in his room, sulking
When Mom checks, the teen
explains that he has lost his phone
Mom helps find it in the messy room
"Why didn't you just look?" she says

An old man sits outside the shelter, freezing
When the worker peers out, the old man
explains that he has nowhere to sleep
Worker opens the door wider, lets him in
"Why didn't you just knock?" he says

If our child or neighbor needs something
and we, imperfect parents, impatient people
give them what they need,
why wouldn't God, perfect, patient Parent
answer our needs?

We sit, crying, sulking, cold in so many ways
When God sits next to us
He explains that He is always there to help
Ask. Seek. Knock.
So simple

Matthew 7:12

ONE RULE

This is perhaps
the most profound verse in the Bible

How would you like to be treated?
With love? kindness? respect?

How would you like to be treated?
As though you can be trusted?
someone with something to say?
an equal?

How would you like to be treated?
With charity when you meet misfortune?
compassion when you need comfort?
gentleness when you have done wrong?

How would you like to be treated?
As though you have worth?
someone beautiful inside and out?
a child of God?

Treat others like that
Give them a true gift

What a stunning world
if we all followed this One Rule

Matthew 7:13

THE ROAD HOME

do not follow crowds
on wide highways. Follow Christ
on slim, Light-filled paths

Matthew 7:24-27

STORMY SEASONS

Hurricane winds howl, shake the house
Rain pounds windows, roars to be let in

Nervous, unsure of what I need
I open the Bible for comfort
not looking for any particular page

Book falls open to The Two Foundations
        Rain? Yes
        Wind? Yes
        Solid?

A solid foundation?

In times of despair
In times of desperation
In times of heartache
In times of hurricane-strength problems …
Do I doubt?

It's easy enough to praise God when things are going well

What about when the air swirls and debris flies
        when disaster taunts
        when friends desert
        when illness strikes
        when bills overwhelm
        when we can see nothing but the storm

Let's build a foundation of faith
to hold us up during times of doubt
Let's climb higher and find our footing on Solid Rock

Forget the storm
We are warm in His Love
Wild winds will not scare us

Matthew 8:23-26

WHERE IS OUR FAITH?

Jesus is so secure
in His Father's love
that nothing worries Him

We cry, "Save us!"
but what we really mean is
"Save us from doubt!"

Let's not ask God for protection
so much as for faith
Then we will sleep soundly

knowing God is with us
knowing Jesus is with us
knowing the Spirit is with us

and that will make
all the difference
in how we live

Matthew 9:35-36

COMPASSION

Jesus was "moved with pity"
Moved with pity for us
He ached for us
He was troubled by our trouble
He preached and He cured and He blessed
    and yet
Jesus knew He would not reach
    everyone
And His heart hurt
How can *we* not be touched
by Someone who loves us that much?

Matthew 10:28

WE WILL BE OKAY

We will be okay
Even if our bodies are bruised
    if our bodies die
God's love will remain

We are afraid of violence
And we should be
    we should find
peaceful ways to stop it

We are afraid of violence
But we must remember
    we must understand
that no one can touch our souls

Our souls belong to God
But our bodies belong to earth
    our bodies will return to dust
while our souls sing for eternity

Let your soul sing
And let your voice be heard
    let no one stop you
from showing kindness to all

God's love will remain
Even if our bodies die
    if our bodies are bruised
we will be okay

Matthew 10:37
CONFUSING CONDITIONS

Jesus had some conditions
that can be confusing
How can you love anyone
more than you love your parents
or your children?
How can that be?
Jesus is not asking that you
lock yourself away in prayer
and ignore your family
It's the opposite
If you love Jesus
truly, unequivocally
You will love others even more
than you do now
You can't help it

Loving Jesus
makes you look at the world differently
Feeling His love
makes you more willing to forgive
You will have more patience
with friends and family
and more patience with yourself
It's hard to be good some days
sometimes especially to those we love most
Jesus sees we need help
That's what his "conditions" mean
If you put Him first
you will love others even more
than you do now
You can't help it

Matthew 11:28-30
COME TO ME

Come to me ...
An invitation
An invitation
      to be free from worry
      to take a deep breath
      to learn to be humble
      to heal hearts with rest

Come to me ...
An invitation
An invitation
      to release all grudges
      to find our purpose
      to let Someone guide us
      to seek greater Love

Come to me ...
An invitation
An invitation
      to follow the good path
      to ease heavy loads
      to discover real joy
      to find lasting peace

I think I'll RSVP

Matthew 12:1-14
MERCY, NOT SACRIFICE

The pharisees loved the law
more than they loved God or fellow man
   loved condemning more than saving
   loved tricking more than guiding
   loved looking holy more than being holy

When common sense whispers what is right, listen
That's Jesus speaking mercy and love
to your heart

Matthew 12:46-50
FAMILY

It may seem callous
that Jesus ignores
His natural family
in this passage

Look deeper
Jesus loves His family
What He is saying is
that we are all family

When you hurt someone
you hurt a child of God
When you love someone
you love a child of God

Jesus shows no favoritism
We must work toward peace
as brothers and sisters
All as children of God

Matthew 13:1-23

SCATTERING SEED

Scattering seed
    Some falls on paths
        eaten by birds
    We hear the Word
    but do not listen
Scattering seed
    Some falls on rocks
        grows, then dies
    We hear the Word
    but do not let it into our hearts
Scattering seed
    Some falls on thorns
        grows, then chokes
    This is most of us (if we are honest)
    We allow worldly cares to smother the Word
Scattering seed
    Some falls on soil
        grows, is nourished, reaches for Light
    We listen, the Word seeps deep
    We plant Goodness, harvest Faith

Matthew 13:24-30

THE HARVEST

We seek justice when someone wrongs us
We wonder why God does not intervene

He will, but in His time, not ours
There is injustice in the world, not in heaven

For now, we do our best to grow with the wheat
The Gardener will deal with the weeds

Matthew 14:22-33
KEEP WALKING

It's easy to believe that
Jesus
Son of God
walked on water
But how did Peter?

Faith
As long as Peter
kept his eyes on
Jesus
He was fine

But when Peter
looked at the troubles
surrounding him
—strong wind, choppy waves, deep sea—
he faltered, sank

Keep your eyes on
Jesus
Faith
will give you courage
to keep walking

Matthew 15:32-39
FEEDING THE WORLD

We want to keep
what we have for ourselves
      Feed someone
      You won't go hungry
We want to save it
in case we need it
      Feed someone
      You won't go hungry
We don't have much and
we earned what we have
      Feed someone
      You won't go hungry
We can't feed the thousands
Jesus fed with a few fish, a bit of bread
But can we feed one person?
Can we give one meal?
What if we each helped one other person—just one?
Would there be a hungry person left?

Matthew 18:1-5
THE GREATEST

In our world
the greatest are
the rich and powerful
the rough and tough leaders
the bold, famous names
recognizable

In God's world
the greatest are
the peaceful and gentle
the trusting followers
the faithful unknown
eyes on God alone

Matthew 19:1-9

DIVORCE

"What God has joined together
no human being must separate"

True

But sometimes it is not God joining people
Sometimes
People make mistakes and choose poorly

Do not discard a marriage
Do not treat your vows as empty promises
Be good to one another
Respect one another
Honor your soul mate

If, however,
Your partner uses you, abuses you
If
Your relationship is dangerous, poisonous
If
Your spouse has broken the marriage
by breaking vows
by refusing to get sober
by crushing your spirit
by committing acts that cannot be undone

Then
You have every right to be free
God knows your heart
Why would He not want you happy?

Matthew 19:13-15
NEED
A PICK-ME-UP?

envision Jesus
welcoming, blessing children
smiling all the while

Matthew 19:23-30
START TODAY

We hear it all the time
"You can't take it with you"
But we continue to value
wealth above people
Why not start on the path
to heaven by giving away?

Buy blankets
for the shelter
Buy extra groceries
for the family on food stamps
Buy a cup of tea
for the friend who is stressed
Buy a case of canned food
for the soup kitchen shelves
Buy extra school supplies
for a teacher to give a child

Give, even if it is a smile
or holding the door open
or calling your mom
Why not start on the path
—your path—
today?

Matthew 20:1-16

ENVY

Why do we compare ourselves
with those who have more

Why not compare ourselves
with those who have less

Stop wanting
Start thanking
Stop whining
Start caring

Matthew 20:17-19

PREDICTION

You're in your early thirties
You have food, family, friends
You live life doing what you love,
traveling, helping others
You teach. You heal. You love.
When you sleep, it is a deep, guiltless sleep
You awake refreshed, ready to live another day

You enjoy life

Could you knowingly let all that go,
walk willingly to your death—
a torturous, excruciatingly painful death—
because your Father asked you?

Matthew 20:29-34
GREAT FAITH

People warned them
to be quiet
With great faith
they got louder
They knew the power
of people was limited

They believed the power
of Jesus was not

They were right

The people who warned them
must have been astonished
After all, wasn't their blindness
a clear sign
that they or their parents
were sinners being punished?

Don't let negative people
quiet your faith

Jesus hears you

Matthew 21:6-9
JERUSALEM

What an entry—
like a great president!
or returning hero!
How Jerusalem welcomed,
adored this man of God!

Jesus knew most
would turn from Him,
mock Him, demand His death

And yet, He stuck to
His mission with
determination, humility, Love

If we can apply His example
to a tiny portion of our lives …
If we can take care of others
despite the fact that they
may hurt or betray us …
If we can live in the present …
If we can find ways to help …
If we can sympathize …
Empathize …
We will learn a little
of what it feels like to Love

Matthew 21:12-14

ACTION

Some people have a problem
imagining a peace-loving Jesus
overturning tables
Not me. I love that side of Him
That side shows Jesus was human
That side shows that emotions
sometimes get the best of us
Jesus exposed their actions as wrong
treating the temple as a marketplace
lowering a place of worship to a level
of greed and profit. Notice that
He hurt no one—so important
He merely cleared the way for people
to come to Him and be healed

Matthew 21:28-32

EXPECTATION

God does not expect us to be perfect
He knows we are stubborn
   knows we can do stupid things
But God does not expect us
to stay in the dark forever either
At some point
God expects us to notice a distant Light
and follow it
   follow Him
At some point
God expects us to recognize Truth
and understand that He is Love
   understand that our actions, not words only,
determine our heavenly future
and give us a sense of inner peace
an inner peace that we can have now

Matthew 22:23-30

HEAVEN

We have no idea
what heaven is like
what the end is like

No marriages?
No families?
No favorites?

It's because we will all
be one. There will be

No jealousy
No evil
No pride

We will be united in Love
and all the pointless trivialities
we thought so vitally important

on earth
Will vanish

Matthew 22:34-40

THE GREATEST
COMMANDMENTS

it's all about Love
Love God and Love each other ...
a world-changing plan

Matthew 23:1-7

PAUSE

We may be cheering for Jesus
as He tells off the scribes
as He puts the pharisees in their place
But we've all played that game
condemning someone's actions
while committing the same sins
None of us are blameless
and we need to remember
that God will judge the hypocrites

Are you one? Do some soul-searching
What can you change about yourself?

Find one thing, one small thing
you can change to be more
like Christ
And when you've managed to make that change
Find another small thing, one small thing
you can change to be more
like Christ
Seeing faults of others on public display
should not make us feel superior or smug

It should make us pause and ask
"Am I like that? What can I change?"

Matthew 24:35
ONLY THE WORD ENDURES

Nothing lasts
Nothing
not your home
not your money
not your body
And one day
Earth will be gone
Heaven will be gone
Heaven will be gone
Nothing
will separate us from
the words of Jesus
the Word
the Love
The Love
will end, mend
all differences
between us
The Word of God
endures
eternally

Matthew 24:36
WE DO NOT KNOW

Forget the doomsday "prophets"
who "interpret" the Bible
and "see" the signs
and "know" the day—
The End of the World!

Jesus tells us only our Father
            our Father alone
decides

That's good enough for me
to ignore "predictions"
and go on living my life
the best that I can

Matthew 24:42-51
TO CONTINUE

So …
If we do not know
when the end is coming—
not of the world
not of our bodies—
we are free to live
       free from fear
But …
If we do not know
when the end is coming—
not of the world
not of our bodies—
we must also live in love
       live for God
Do you really want to meet God
right after you
       have been mean to someone
       have cheated
       have lied
       have stolen
       have hurt a loved one
       have judged someone harshly
Do you really want to meet God
and have Him treat you the way
you've just mistreated another?

Wouldn't you rather die
with a prayer on your lips
praising God for the day
thanking God for the gifts in your life

Wouldn't you rather die
helping a neighbor
preparing a family meal
letting someone else go first in line
ignoring the driver who cut you off
saying something kind

Wouldn't you rather die
forgiving someone
making the tough, but right, decision
telling your spouse or child or parent or friend
that you love him or her
that you value his or her presence in your life

Well ...
Wouldn't you?

Matthew 25:14-25
WELL DONE

Well done, my good and faithful servant
I can't imagine any better words

God gives each of us different gifts
—wildly varied, unique, wonderful gifts—
so that we may all contribute in some way
We are given what we can handle
We are expected to use these gifts
doing what we are meant to do
to help bring goodness, happiness, healing
to ourselves and others
Is it hard?
You bet
We might get tired
We might have to crawl over obstacle after obstacle
We might have to search our hearts daily
to ask if we are on the right road
We might have to push ourselves to keep going
keep trying, studying, working
especially when
we feel like throwing away our gifts
or burying them
We can't let our fears or insecurities win
We need to get up, face each day
and do our best
to share our gifts

And one day we may hear
Well done, my good and faithful servant

Matthew 25:34-36

IS THAT ALL IT TAKES?

Feed a hungry child
Welcome a stranger
Clothe those in need
Care for someone sick
Visit a lonely prisoner

Inherit
Everlasting Life

Matthew 26:6-11

THE GIFT

Again we return to judging
Judging others
When someone does something
     with good intentions, genuine
what right do we have to say
     the money should have been spent differently
     the person should have acted differently
     the gift should have been given differently

Let's save judgment for something
     evil, violent
In fact
Let's save judgment
for God

Matthew 26:14-16

WHAT WOULD YOU DO FOR MONEY?

What if someone paid you five dollars
to steal a car?
No?
What if it were one million
to steal a pack of gum?
Two million to trash the name of someone innocent?
Three million to hurt, not kill, someone?

Do you dip into the company's petty cash jar?
Do you go home with the hotel towels?
Have you blamed someone for your mistake
so as not to lose your money-making job
or the valued respect of a family member?
Has greed for something you wanted
ever pushed you to leave a friend in need?

Here's a little trick to help you
become a better person
When you do something
—even the littlest thing—
ask yourself Why
(without justifying)
If you feel good about
the answer you get, you're set

If not ...

Matthew 26:26-28

DINING WITH JESUS

They were with Him each day
Walked with Jesus from town to town
Witnessed healings, miracles
Listened to Him with wonder
And yet, to His disciples,
This was an ordinary Passover meal
The words Jesus spoke that night
Were beyond them
They could not wrap their minds around
the meaning of the Bread as Body, Body as Bread
       the Cup as Blood, Blood as Cup
Forgiveness of sins?
What?

Would we understand any better now
If Jesus were to show up at our door
If He were to sit and eat
Repeat the same words?

Maybe, like His original disciples,
The full, complete, underlying, ultimate meaning
Would elude us

But they gave thanks
That much they understood
That much we can do, too

Matthew 26:31-35

FRIENDSHIP DENIED

Have you ever promised a friend
you'd stand by her no matter what
and then avoided, abandoned her
out of fear of association
        fear of reputation
                fear of retaliation?

Peter wanted to stand by his friend
but fear got in the way

Jesus gets that we are weak
Ask Him to walk by your side
Ask to borrow His strength
So you can stand by your friend
        stand by your promise
                stand by what's right

Matthew 26:36-44

AGONY

Sometimes you don't
want to do
        something
but know you should

Take this
        something
you don't want to do
and put it into perspective
Is it really such a big deal, this
        something?
Pray. Search your heart
It can't always be about us
Sometimes we have to put
friends and family
first

In light of the
        something
Jesus did
is your
        something
such a terrible sacrifice?

Matthew 26:62-64

SPEAK

Stay silent when you
should. Speak the truth when you must
Do not be afraid

Matthew 27:21-26

DO NOT GIVE IN

Pilate succumbed to
politics, power, pressure
Pray that you do not

Matthew 27:27-66

CRUCIFIXION

Mocked, beaten
Bruised, bleeding
Alone, frightened
Pain heightened

Name scorned
Veil torn
An earthquake
The heartbreak

From Mary's womb
To Joseph's tomb
Guards brought
Truth sought

Matthew 28
RESURRECTION

Jesus came back from the dead
Just as He had promised
And still, it was hard for His
Followers to comprehend
They were afraid. They were joyful
They doubted. They trusted
Their emotions were a boat
Rocking high and low on the sea
Thrown and tossed and scared
Yet exhilarated, filled with wonder
And aren't we all like that?
Faith-filled days when we praise
Dark-doubt nights when we question
That's how it works—we're human

But every so often, stop

Let the words of Jesus
Find a place in your heart
I am with you always
Take a deep breath
See Him before you
Saying those words
I am with you always
Feel strength and comfort
On faith-filled days
On dark-doubt nights
I am with you always
Welcome the words
Welcome the promise of the
Resurrection

Mark 1:4-8
AMBASSADORS

The church, the priests
The holy brothers and sisters
are ambassadors, agents
spokespersons, delegates

Like John
they can guide us
inspire us
preach and teach us

Learn from them but
keep looking Higher, too
It's God's blessing we seek
not man's

Mark 2:1-5
STATUS

He was lowered
through the roof—
something a frenzied fan
of a rock star might do

In fact …

What if we assigned
Jesus rock-star status,
trying everything possible
to be near Him?

Mark 3:1-6
WHY?

Jesus could not understand
the hardened hearts
of the pharisees any more
than He can understand
our hardened hearts
when we do not feel
compassion for others

Mark 3:23-25
TOGETHER

Let go
of petty arguments
We will never all have
the same opinion
We are individuals
with our own ways
of seeing things

Focus on the common goal
Focus on
      helping the poor
      loving the lonely
      comforting the grieving
      hugging a child
      saying something kind

Let's unite
when someone needs our help
Arguing over silly differences
divides us, makes us weak
We stay strong
and do the most good
Together

Mark 4:30-32
START SMALL

it is fine to start
with the tiniest of faith
give it time to grow

Mark 5:25-34
GET CLOSER

She felt if she could just touch Jesus
she would be cured
And she was

Getting closer to Jesus will not hurt you
but it may save you
Why not give it a try?

You can get closer by
      reading the Bible
      reading inspirational books
      praying, thanking, meditating
      acting toward someone as Jesus would
      finding a way to forgive yourself

Try it
Feel His healing goodness
rush through you

Take a step—just one
Jesus wants to help
He loves you

Mark 6:17-29
DON'T SAY WHAT YOU
DON'T MEAN

Herod promised his niece/stepdaughter
she could have anything she asked
He did not expect her request
but gave her John's head—
he had sworn so to guests

Not everyone will trick you
but what is the point anyway
of making boastful oaths?
In all matters, from
tiny idea to grand plan,

Think before you speak
You'll save yourself
much grief

Mark 8:11-12
SIGNS

signs that God loves us
are in the beauty of the
world and in our hearts

Mark 12:41-44
YOU HAVE SO MUCH TO GIVE

She was poor
She was alone
She chose to give

Are you tired?
Are you sad?
Choose to smile

Are you hurt?
Are you mad?
Choose to forgive

Are you dying?
Are you scared?
Choose to visit the sick

Are you selfish?
Are you stubborn?
Choose to change

Are you late?
Are you rushed?
Choose to be patient

Are you broke?
Are you discouraged?
Find someone who has less

Choose to give

Mark 16:1-6

EMPTY

empty the tomb of
your heart; make room for Peace, Light ...
Forgiveness of self

Luke 1:31-37

NOTHING IS IMPOSSIBLE

When money is tight
and the bills are piling up
Have hope and remember
Nothing is impossible for God

When a loved one is ill or hurt
and the prognosis is not good
Have hope and remember
Nothing is impossible for God

When an injustice has been done
and you are fighting for your rights
Have hope and remember
Nothing is impossible for God

When the atrocities mount
and peace looks unattainable
Have hope and remember
Nothing is impossible for God

Things won't always turn out
the way we want or
the way we think they should
But we have to hold onto hope
and remember
Nothing is impossible for God

Luke 1:38
HIS HANDMAID

If God were to whisper a plan to your heart
And that plan involved
>tremendous faith
>possible ridicule
>potential divorce
>false accusations
>threat of death

How many of us would say yes?

Think of the strength, the courage
>of Mary's unhesitant response

Each day
>in honor of Mary's decision,
Try to do something small
>but right

Give up your seat on the bus after a long day
Let someone with cranky kids go ahead of you
Shovel your neighbor's walk after a snow
Bring home a tiny gift for your children
Let your spouse choose the TV show
Call your dad
Invite someone to dinner
Make a donation
Volunteer
Respond to rudeness with kindness

These acts will prepare you
should God ask something more
And even if He doesn't
These acts will fill you
with Peace, Purity, Security
because in your heart you will know
You are part of God's plan

Luke 1:5-20 and 57-64

A SECOND CHANCE

It's natural to question—
especially things that are
so amazing
that they are
hard to believe …
Was Zechariah punished?
Not God's style

Zechariah was silenced
to allow him
to contemplate, to pray
to ponder, to wonder
And when the time came
Zechariah knew the answer
because he had accepted it fully
in his heart

And when we accept Truth fully
in our hearts
We, too, find many ways
distinct ways
to communicate Truth
to bless God
with actions and words and talents

Zechariah had a second chance
and he took it

What will you do with yours?

Luke 2:1-7

NO ROOM AT THE INN

How many times have you grumbled
about the unfairness of it all …
Doing something you do not want to do
Going somewhere you do not want to be

I have—and far too often
But at some point we take a breath, say
"Okay, God. I'll do it.
But only because I have no choice."
And *then*
God asks something even harder on top of that!
My response is
"Oh, come on, God! I did everything you asked.
Why is this happening to *me*?"

Not Mary and Joseph
They had to travel, so they did
She was nine months pregnant, but she went
It was time to give birth, so they looked for a place
And *then*
No one would let them in!

My response is to whine when the washing
machine breaks and there is a mountain of snow
to shovel and the toilet overflows and everyone needs
something and my day is too crazy to have a second to myself

Mary's response was to do what she had to do
without complaining
Joseph's response was to support Mary
without complaining

Maybe it's time for me to
Complain a little less
Count blessings a little more
and
Do what I have to do

Luke 2: 8-18
YOU COUNT

Ever feel like you're
not worth much?
Your job is not important
You are not rich
No one asks your opinion
in matters of high value

When Jesus was born
Shepherds were the lowest
Doing a "dirty" job
Not respected, not admired
and the angels appeared
to *them*

The shepherds didn't wait
They went to see this child
They praised this child
They shared the message
of the angels
not caring what anyone
thought of them

They counted
You count
We all count—
Including the
people you think
are somehow
"beneath" *you*

Luke 2:19
HOLD IT IN YOUR HEART

Whenever anyone spoke
of her child and the
wondrous things He would do
Mary held it in her heart

Whenever you hear
of a kindness and see
goodness in things people do
Hold it in your heart

Look for these treasures everywhere
in something your spouse says or does
or your children, coworkers, strangers
Hold every charity in your heart

It will give you strength
against the evil in the world
It will help you face
awfulness with Love

Luke 2:41-52

WHERE WERE YOU?

Have you ever lost sight of your child
at a store or fair or park?
Then you know how terrifying it is
Think of Mary's and Joseph's panic
as they went from person to person
and no one had seen their child
A day of asking
A day of traveling back
Three days before finding Him
Perhaps it's the closest thing to a reprimand
that Jesus ever got from His worried mother

Jesus did not understand why His parents
did not know where He would be
Jesus did understand their concern
and did not cause them worry again
Mary did not understand why her Son
had stayed behind in the temple
Mary did understand that it was
one more thing she should hold in her heart

Find one more thing
to hold in your heart today

Luke 4:16-30
REJECTION

You come up with a great idea
Something as simple as a new meal
Or as complex as a new business
But friends and family do not agree

That you are onto something

Maybe your husband laughs at your recipe
Asks that you stick to the old stuff
Maybe a neighbor thinks being a musician
Is a hobby, not a plan, nothing serious

And it hurts

Jesus expected, accepted cynicism
He did not hold it against them
Jesus just moved past them
And went on with His work

Luke 6:35-36
LOVE YOUR ENEMY

why should we do good,
be kind, merciful? because
God does that for us

Luke 7:1-10
SAY THE WORD

The officer was a gentile and knew
Jesus, a Jew, would consider him unclean
and would not enter his house

Jesus would have, but the officer's faith
was so great that there was no need

"Say the word," the officer pleaded

He understood his servant would be healed
by the Word of Jesus alone—and he was

Let's start repeating that act of faith

Say the word and I will get past this
Say the word and I will find a solution
Say the word and I will welcome hope again
Say the word and I will let You into my heart

Luke 7:28-35

AM I MARVELOUS?

When we read about the pharisees
not believing the message
of John the Baptist
not believing the good news
of Jesus the Christ
We may say that *we*
would have been smart enough
to recognize the greatness of both

But read on
Jesus compares the people of that day
to children
Jesus compares them
not to the innocent children He welcomes
but to spoiled, egocentric brats
"We played the flute for you, but you did not dance"

Humph!
Why weren't you paying attention
to how marvelous I am?
We are all a bit like that
I want to be a good person
and have faith and I want
you to *notice* and tell me
I am better than others!
But it doesn't work like that

We need to do the best we can
Trust God, help others, follow our hearts
Do the right thing
without expectation
without commendation
It is nice to be recognized
(We are, after all, human)
but do not let it be a condition
of your faith and kindness—
please?

Luke 7:37-48

ARE YOUR SINS TOO GREAT TO BE FORGIVEN?

Think you've done too much harm
        to be forgiven?
Listen to me
There is nothing, nothing that you have done
        that God will not forgive
Don't use your past errors
        as reasons to keep sinning
Listen to me
If your child does something wrong
        would you rather she keep doing it or
        would you rather she stop
                so you can hold her and tell her
                "It's okay now"
Listen to me
God loves you
        When you do something wrong, pray
        Instead of watching you repeat your mistakes
                He wants to hold you and say
                "It's okay now"

Luke 13:34

BE WILLING

We've heard the comparison, Jesus as shepherd
But Jesus as hen?
And yet, it touches me
    The Divine gathering Her baby chicks
    Protecting them under Her wings
The only reason it doesn't happen?
    We say no
Be willing to see Jesus, God, Holy Spirit in any form
What gives you the most comfort?
Can you picture God singing you a lullaby?
The Holy Spirit sending a soft breeze?
Jesus walking by your side?
    Then let it happen

Luke 17:1-2

EVEN WORSE
THAN SINNING

Even worse than sinning
is tempting someone else
to sin
Why would you ask
another
to join you in
doing something
you know is wrong?

When you face God
you will have to answer
for your sins
You really will not want
to explain
why you taught
someone else
to make the same
bad choices

Thinking of
tempting someone?
Don't
Tempting someone now?
Stop
Tempted someone in the past?
Apologize
Ask forgiveness from
that person
You can do it

Luke 19:1-10

DO WHATEVER IT TAKES

Zacchaeus had to see Jesus!
He knew life would get better
if he could only see Him
But the crowd was thick
and Z was short
That did not stop him
Z climbed a tree
He cared not what anyone thought

Be unconventional!
Find a way to get to Jesus
and He will say to you, too,
"I must stay at your house!"
The joy Z felt!
Jesus accepted him
in spite of everything he had done
Tax collectors were cheaters
who collected more than owed
who got rich by robbing others

But Z was done with that life!
He was so happy, so thankful
to be given the chance
to make things right
And the self-righteous
who disapproved of Jesus
hanging out with a sinner?
Both Z and Jesus ignored
those stuck-up snobs
Jesus' job was and is to find the lost

Welcome back, Z!
Welcome back to all who
Do Whatever It Takes
to find Jesus in their hearts
and begin again
to do what is good in His sight

Luke 22:47-51

BETRAYED

We've all been there
The friend who whispered behind our back
The coworker who took credit for our project
The names we were called unjustly
The false accusations, the broken promises
It hurts. It just about kills us
It empties us, breaks us

Jesus took Judas into His care
Walked with him, taught him
Loved him
Maybe it would have hurt less
If Judas had screamed
"There he is! Get him!"
But a kiss?

And yet
All I can picture
Are eyes of pity, compassion
As Jesus looks at Judas
Not only does Jesus accept arrest
But He heals the servant's ear
He takes time in this moment
In this moment of ultimate betrayal
To show Mercy
To call for Peace
Jesus never sees Judas again

No one is asking you
To hang out with your betrayer
But try, as best you can
To forgive
To move on
To pray for Mercy and Peace
For the one who wronged you

Luke 23:39-43

WHICH PERSON WILL YOU BE?

Two criminals, one
sneers, the other believes; which
person will you be?

There is time to change
Rearrange your life, ask the
way to Paradise

Luke 24:13-16

DO YOU KNOW HIM?

He was the elderly gentleman
who held open the door
when our arms were full
but we were too rushed
to murmur a simple thank-you

She was the tired new mother
with a crying child
and instead of offering comfort
we sighed loudly, glancing at her with annoyance

He was the careful 16-year-old
who looked both ways before going
after the light turned green
while we blasted the horn
immediately, impatiently

She was the cashier working two jobs
to feed her children
and we snapped at her for not
packing the groceries the "right" way

He was the employee
following the rules
so he wouldn't get fired
yet we yelled at him
as if he enjoyed saying no

She was the grieving spouse
who lost her life's love last week
but we did not ask why
she was on a park bench crying; she was not our problem

We have all met Him
If we had known
it was Jesus
would we have acted
differently?

John 1:1
THE WORD

This is how it began

The Word is Truth
       and Beauty
The Word is Grace
       and Goodness
The Word is Justice
       and Equality

The Word is Jesus
The Word is God
The Word is Spirit
The Word is Love

John 1:19-27
MESSENGERS

Never be so full of yourself
that you forget Who gave you your gifts
Humility goes a long way in all things
     personal relationships
     business deals
     social justice
     celebrity status
Yes, we work hard to achieve things
But remember, the grace of God
made these accomplishments possible
Like John, we can divert the attention
away from ourselves and direct it
to our source of Goodness and Light
Then we, too, will be messengers of Truth

John 2:1-5

HE WALKED AMONG US

I often think about
the water into wine
I understand it was the first
of His signs, so it's significant
and Jesus performed signs
because people needed them

But I also love that Jesus
obeyed His mother in that
moment
Did she know His mission was
to start?
Did she give her Son a little push?

And I love that Jesus
was at a wedding
drinking wine
spending time with friends, family

He was not a down, dejected person
Jesus celebrated life
smiling, laughing
sharing the Good News
of a loving Father
of a heaven waiting

Don't misunderstand me
Jesus did not run around
drinking, gambling
living for pleasure
But He did accept and appreciate
being human

How much greater that makes
His sacrifice for us
knowing the way His days here
would end

John: 3:16-17

FOR GOD SO
LOVED
THE WORLD

There is no
sweeter passage
in the Bible
Jesus came to save
not condemn
God sent His Son
out of pure Love
Redemption and Love
Love and Redemption
Read these verses
Let them
sing to your soul
Let them find a home
in your heart
Let them settle
into your very being
For God
so loved
the world …
For God
SO LOVED
us

John 4:39-42

FORGET EVERYTHING BUT FAITH

How did you come to be reading this book—
this book of poems?
How did you come to be reading this book—
the Bible?
Maybe your family introduced you to Faith
Maybe it was a friend
or a priest or someone on TV
or someone you overheard on the street
However you got here is not the point
It's what you do with Faith now
You must believe for yourself—
not because someone suggested it

Forget everything you've heard or learned
Forget these poems
Forget even the Bible

What do you believe?

Faith is between you and God—
no one else
It does not depend on family
or friends or words or beauty
or priests or rabbis or imams
or jobs or intelligence
or understanding

What do *you* believe?
What does *your* heart say?

John 6:35

THE BREAD OF LIFE

It's easy to understand
that only spiritual Love
can satisfy us
It's also easy to forget

We get so caught up
in making a living
in accusations and blame
in idiotic quarrels
We get so caught up
in collecting objects
in destroying reputations
in bloody, meaningless wars

We forget that our only purpose
is to follow the living example
of Jesus, of Love
Our only purpose
is to allow ourselves to be filled
with the Bread of Life
with the Goodness that sustains us
and gives us the determined ability
to live in peace—or at least to try

One day all our needs will be met
in a way they never can be on earth
no physical hunger, no fear
no violence, no spiritual thirst
Give yourself permission to envision
this future
Live as if it is almost here

John 8:3-11

THE BRILLIANT, COMPASSIONATE RESPONSE

I find this to be one of the
most powerful passages in the Bible
She committed adultery. She sinned
She harmed herself and her family
She was at fault. She was to blame
The LAW commanded she be stoned
to death
How RIGHTEOUS they felt
shoving her before Jesus, testing His response
He would have no choice
but to agree to stoning the sinner

"Let the one among you who is without sin
be the first to throw a stone at her."

Could there have been a response
more brilliant, compassionate?
Whenever I begin to feel superior
I read this again and remember
I am no better than anyone else
I am no less than anyone else
I read this again and remember
The woman was given a chance
to start over, to begin again
I ask God's forgiveness for judging
I start over, begin again

John 8:31-32

FREEDOM

To be truly Free is to answer to Truth
To answer to Truth is to seek God
To seek God is to believe in the Word
To believe in the Word is to find Love
To find Love is to be truly Free

John 9:1-41
WHAT'S NOT TO UNDERSTAND?

Jesus came not to conform, but to shake things up

The man was born "imperfect," meaning he was a sinner
or his parents had sinned, and this was God's punishment
Jesus' answer is matter-of-fact
> *No, he did not sin. No, his parents did not sin*
> *But watch … I am about to reveal God's glory through him*
And Jesus gives the man his sight

Now, of course, every town loves a good scandal
Instead of celebrating, neighbors bring the man to face the pharisees
After all, Jesus performed this work on the sabbath
The man is as matter-of-fact as Jesus
> *He gave me sight*
> *He is a prophet*

They question his parents who say their son can speak for himself—
not because they are proud of him
or because they are happy for him
They are afraid of being tossed out of the synagogue

Again the man is summoned. Again he responds matter-of-factly
> *Jesus has to have been sent by God*
> *Otherwise, He could not have cured me*
And so, the pharisees bluster rather than listen
They call him a sinner and toss him out

Now comes my favorite part
Jesus hears about this and goes back to him
He does not simply "perform a sign" and move on
Jesus really opens his eyes, reveals Himself as the Son of Man

Now comes the important part: The man believes Jesus
The pharisees are unconvinced.
Clarification: They refuse to be convinced
They jeer at the honest, open, trusting response of the once-blind man
They choose to remain blind out of stubbornness, pride, fear

John 11:17-35

JESUS WEPT

Though Jesus understood better than anyone
that death on earth is not the end
He still wept when He saw His friends weeping

Jesus cries with you when you are in pain
It saddens Him to see you suffer
At those times when you feel most lost?

Jesus is holding you close

John 13:5-17

JESUS WASHES THEIR FEET

At first Peter refuses
because he thinks this act is
beneath the dignity
of one as great as Jesus
and only agrees when Jesus says he must
Peter is still confused
but Jesus knows there is no better lesson
than His example
   We need to carry out our work—
   whatever work that may be—
   with grace and humility
If we think we are "too good"
to "lower" ourselves to help someone
or to complete some "menial" task,
then we should give some thought
to the meaning of "good"
and recall the living example of Christ
who is not a historical figure
but walks with us, guides us today

John 13:34-35

LOVE ONE ANOTHER

There is only one way
to show you are Christian
Act as Christ would act
There is only one way
to act as Christ would act
Love everyone—not some or most
or only those who love you
Love everyone
      the rude one, the condescending boss, the spouse who
      lost patience with you this morning, the teen who
      talked back, the person who stole your identity, the man who
      raped your daughter, the woman who killed your child,
      the terrorist—domestic or international

Jesus did not say it would be easy

John 14:2

IMAGINE

Jesus has prepared
a place in heaven, a place
that is just for you

John 15:4

THE BRANCH

Break off a branch
and it will no longer bear fruit
because it has nothing to sustain it

Break away from Love
and you will no longer bear love
because you've left the One who sustains you

Picture branches brittle, bare, cracked, snapped
from their life-giving Source
fruit rotting in the eerie emptiness

Picture branches healthy, green, fresh, connected
to their life-giving Source
hanging heavy with fruit and Love

John 17:4

HOW TO REALLY GLORIFY GOD

We are all here for a reason
and have only a season to finish it
In your heart you know what God asks

Maybe He wants you to be a mechanic
who works hard to get cars back on the road
He could have called you to be a hairdresser
who makes people feel beautiful
Perhaps He has asked you to be a teacher
who knows education is an incredible gift
Are you a custodian
who works behind the scenes?
Are you a farmer
who never has a day off?
Are you a stay-at-home parent
who is not appreciated by those who work for pay?

Maybe you, the mechanic,
have fixed a flat tire for free
for the senior on a fixed income
And you, the hairdresser,
make and give wigs
to those with cancer
Probably you, the teacher,
give up your free time
to tutor or coach or mentor
Has anyone noticed that you, the custodian,
clean up the worst messes without complaint?
And you, the farmer,
leave a bit of every crop behind for the poor?
Or you, the stay-at-home parent,
give up material things to be with your child?

God sees you doing His work
You are glorifying Him during your short time here
Have faith that He sees

John 16:2
PRAY FOR THEM

We live in an age
when terrorists believe
they are glorifying God by killing
Do not hate them
Pray for them
Pray for peace and understanding
in their hearts

Like those who killed the early Christians
they think they are carrying out God's plan
They don't know that God is Love
and hatred won't help them to know that
Pray for them
Practice kindness
Be the Love that sets them free

John 20:24-29
THOMAS

I don't blame Thomas
I don't think Jesus did either
After all, he had seen his Teacher die
and must have thought his grief-stricken friends were hallucinating
Unlike Thomas, we cannot examine the wounds of the crucifixion
But we can see the signs of the presence of Jesus
everywhere
      —strangers rushing to aid others in times of tragedy
      —someone forgiving the unforgivable
      —people donating kidneys and blood and bone marrow
      —a person dying, saving a friend
      —or even a smile or hug given freely to comfort
We don't have to see Jesus to Believe

Acts 1:6-11

WHY ARE YOU LOOKING AT THE SKY?

Like the apostles who looked
into the air for Jesus
We gaze upward
looking for signs of heaven

But Jesus is not sitting on a throne of clouds
And heaven does not exist at a certain height

The Love of Jesus surrounds us always
Heaven is a state of Pure Joy
that our limited minds cannot comprehend
... yet

Acts 2:1-13

BABEL IN REVERSE

We began with a common language
but became so full of ourselves
        so convinced we were great by ourselves
                without God's help
                        that He jumbled our speech
                                and scattered us

With the gift of the Holy Spirit
we were humbled and amazed
        that though we spoke different languages
                we heard the same message
                        of Christ's sacrifice
                                and it united us

Acts 2:42-47
A LIVING CHURCH

There are beautiful churches all over the world
Some majestic, some simple
Pews fill with sinners and believers
Some come out of a sense of obligation
Some come to make themselves look good
Some come to thank God

It is this last group that catches my attention
The first church was not a building
It was a group of people praising God
They shared their food, possessions, joy
One did not go home to riches while
Another went home to poverty

They were an example—
A living church
A living faith
Today the church has many manmade rules
The first church had only Jesus' rule:
Love one another

Acts 4:32-35
ENOUGH FOR ALL

No one was needy in that first Christian community
(It bears repeating. One poem won't do)

We have enough to share
There is always someone
less fortunate
There is always someone
who would benefit from our abundance

Share your material goods, your money, your time,
your love, your compassion, your faith, your talents
You have something to give
It's not that hard to find *something*
once a year or month or week or day

Ask God to help you act as Jesus would
He will never ask more than you can do—
What a beautiful world
if we all gave
just a little more

Acts 9:1-22; 13:9
SAUL TO PAUL

Stubborn will
Accuser, abuser
Unrelenting, unrepenting
Looking for Christians to kill

to

Persecution done
Anointed, appointed
Unifying, undenying
Loving God's Son

Acts 10:34-35
MANY PATHS

Christians are not superior
God calls *all* who seek Love

If God does not judge
the paths people take
to reach Him
Why do we?

Acts 17:26-28
YOUR HEART

First,
Every human being
          all nationalities, all races
                    came "from one"
It seems obvious that we are equal
          that God loves each of His children
                    with the same fierceness
Sadly, racism still thrives
          Read these verses to erase that
                    from your heart

Second,
We run around
          looking for God
                    desperately seeking Him
He has always been with us
          has always loved us and
                    we exist because God exists
Joyfully, He is near
          Read these verses to embrace that
                    in your heart

Acts 18:9

SPEAK UP, SPEAK OUT

When someone is being bullied, speak up
Racism? Speak out
Intimidation? Speak up
Violence? Speak out
Lies? Speak up
Abuse? Speak out

God called Paul to keep preaching
And He calls some now to keep preaching
But when someone is wronged
God calls *all* to
       Speak UP
       Speak OUT

God does not ask us to shout or swear or call names or become violent
in our defense of another
I don't see that anywhere in His instructions to Paul, do you?
Peacefully, strongly, unrelentingly
       Speak UP
       Speak OUT

And when someone is bullying you, maybe someone will speak up
If someone discriminates against you, maybe someone will speak out
When you are being intimidated, maybe someone will speak up
If someone is hurting you, maybe someone will speak out
When you have been lied to, maybe someone will speak up
If you are being abused, maybe someone will speak out

We can and we will
       Speak UP
       Speak OUT

Acts 20:24
YOUR MINISTRY

How many of us can say
that it does not matter when we die
as long as we have finished
the task the Lord has given us?

We cling to life
We try to prolong it
We are afraid to die
Maybe we should shift our focus to our purpose

Maybe you are called to
      be a good neighbor
            or doctor or mentor
                  or scientist or parent

Whatever you are meant to do
Do it well
We cannot control when we die but
We can control how we *live*

Acts 28:1-2

SHIPWRECKED

Arrested in Jerusalem
Transferred to Caesarea
Imprisoned for two years
Paul was being sent to Rome
when the storm struck
He and the other prisoners and crew
barely made it to the island of Malta

Pretend you live in Malta
You watch cold, hungry, exhausted people
struggling to shore
        some doing their best to swim
        some clinging to the ship's debris
They look frightened and desperate—
But what if it's an act?
What if they mean you harm?

Maybe you should protect your "own" people?

Reading these words
Are you angry with me
for suggesting we block them from entering "our" land?
After all
They are fleeing disaster
If we don't let them in, they will die
They are drenched, drowning, terrified—
Let them in!

The people of Malta did not hesitate
They took care of them
        fed them, sheltered them
        built a fire to warm them
When winter passed, and they were strong enough to sail
The natives not only gave them supplies—
They gave them back their independence, their pride

Maybe we should welcome refugees escaping danger, too?

Romans 2:1
ONE MORE TIME

please hear this once more
you will be judged the same way
that you judge others

Romans 8:18, 31, 38-39
SUFFERING AND HOPE

We all suffer in some way—no one is spared
Yet suffering and hope should always be paired

When these bodies die, we will experience
Love and no pain—joy endless, delirious

Nothing can stop God from sharing His glory
Triumphant ending to every child's story

Romans 8:26-27
IT'S OKAY

You don't know how to pray
That's okay. Neither do I
Simply ask Him to help you endure

We can't put it into words
That's okay. The Spirit translates for us
God hears what we mean

Romans 11:34
TO KNOW GOD'S MIND

is not possible

That's why faith is so important
We cannot understand God's thoughts
or His reasons
Sometimes we have to trust that
He knows what He's doing

Romans 12:2
DO NOT CONFORM

The world is a messed-up place
Willful ignorance
Racism, hatred, violence, war

Don't give in to that
Don't become part of that
Rebel against evil as Jesus did

Look within your heart and mind
Find the inner peace that is God's voice
Don't let the world drag you under

No matter what chaos surrounds you
You possess the power to stand still and
Listen for God's guidance

Romans 12:9-10
BE SINCERE

Don't fake it
Reach deep within
Love others with all you are
Be gentle. Be affectionate. Be grateful
Show mercy. Show respect. Show kindness
Meet their needs with love and humility and
Sincerity

Romans 15:21
WE ARE ALL INVITED

Paul is talking about the gentiles here
acknowledging that Christ came
not only to save the Jewish people
but to save all
By "all," God means ALL
There are many who have never heard of Jesus
who will find everlasting life
There are many of other faiths
who will find everlasting life
There are agnostics
who will find everlasting life
Yes, there are atheists
who will find everlasting life
We don't know their true hearts but

God does

Do what is right and good
Lead by example and then
Let God do the rest
He's got some experience with this

1 Corinthians 10:13

TRUST HIS PLANS FOR YOU

Some days you may be tempted to ask
"Why, God? Why me? I can't do this!"
You want to give up
You need your troubles to end
You are *so tired*

God doesn't give more than you can manage
When you are too exhausted to go on
Let Him carry you for a while
You will overcome your struggles
You will emerge even stronger

1 Corinthians 13:1-3

LOVE—OR NOTHING

if you have all gifts
all things, all wisdom, but no
Love, you have nothing

1 Corinthians 13:4-7

FAVORITE WORDS

Everything you need to know about
Love
is contained in these four simple verses
This short passage speaks about all
Love—love of parents for children, love of
children for parents, romantic love, family
love, neighborly love, love of enemies, love
of those less fortunate and hurting, God's love
for us

If I could only read one part of the Bible each day
These are the verses I would choose
over and over
praying for the words
to make me Whole, make me One with Love

1 Corinthians: 15:58

YOUR WORK WILL BE REMEMBERED

Nothing that you do
for God's glory, for your neighbors
will be forgotten

God will remember each time you were kind
or put someone's needs ahead of yours or
read the Bible or prayed for guidance or made
a decision that brought you closer to peace and
to Him

God may choose to forget your sins but
He will not forget the good you do
God will not forget *you*

2 Corinthians 9:7
NOT *THAT* YOU GIVE, BUT *HOW*

Maybe you're a reluctant giver
You help because you feel you have to
but you grumble

Consider how much nicer it would be
—for us and for them—
if we gave cheerfully?

Galatians 3:28; 4:7
WE ARE THE SAME

We do not choose the country of our birth
or the color of our skin or if we will be disabled
or diseased or falsely imprisoned or enslaved
or viewed as ugly by the world's warped standards

We are the same, you and I
We are one
Unique gifts and personalities? Yes
Different in God's eyes? No

Stop letting the world trick you
into thinking it's you versus me
We are all God's children
finding our way Home

Ephesians 1:16
THE SUBJECT
OF OUR PRAYERS

how often do we
pray for others instead of
solely for ourselves?

Philippians 2:14
POOR ME

This is a hard one
for me
Sometimes I complain
because it makes me
feel holier
that no matter
how bad things get
I keep plugging
staunchly along

But that's a load of crap

I complain
because I like
feeling sorry
for myself
It's nice to think
about a world
where we all do
what we have to do
without whining

Colossians 3:12-14

DRESSING FOR THE DAY

Just as we put on our clothes
We put on our attitude

Arrogance or humility
Kindness or cruelty

Cold-heartedness or gentleness
Tenderness or restlessness

Agitation or serenity
Forgiveness or obscenity

Hatred or Love …
What will you wear this morning?

1 Thessalonians 5:21

KEEP THE GOOD STUFF

Your life is not all put together
Neither is mine
It is fine—required really—
to assess, evaluate, ask questions

Pray, meditate, contemplate …
What are you doing that is good?

Find it
Keep it

Continue to
adjust the not-so-good parts but
embrace with joy the
Good you are most certainly doing

2 Thessalonians 1:6-9

IS THERE A HELL?

The Bible mentions eternal fire
for those who do not repent
I'm not sure about the fire
It's the lines that follow that scare me—
being separated from our Lord, from Love

Hell is a choice
If you don't want to be with God, with Love
He, with great sadness, accepts that
After all, what would be the point
of giving us free will then?

I can't foresee our Father
tossing us away into a pit of despair—
but He won't force us to be with Him either
because that is not Love

And for those who do choose to leave?
I can't fathom
        the empty, aching, *aloneness*
of that Hell

1 Timothy 1:13-16

THE LEARNING CURVE

When we were kids
we did things that were wrong
because we didn't know any better
Gradually we learned what was right
Be nice. Don't hit.
        Be kind. Don't fight.

But have we learned to
Be thankful? Not gossip?
        Be supportive? Not hold grudges?
Has every lesson seeped deeply
into our souls, our everyday routines?
No, we are all—every one of us—still learning

So when God is merciful because
we haven't mastered being good yet
perhaps we should look at this as a lesson, too
Perhaps we should cut others some slack
We all learn different lessons at different times
We are all—every one of us—still in our infancy

One child walks at nine months
One child walks at twelve months
In the end, each runs into loving arms
No matter where you are on the learning curve
God waits for you with mercy
        and outstretched arms

2 Timothy 2:23

CHOOSE YOUR BATTLES

Parents of three-year-olds soon learn
that every "Why?" does not need
an explanation

Answer a child who is sincerely trying
to understand but
When the "Why?" is for attention
it's okay to say (with a hug)
"Because I said so"

Talk with someone who is sincerely trying
to understand but
When someone argues for attention
it's okay to say (with a smile)
"I'm not interested in this debate"

People who encounter foolishness soon learn
that most quarrels do not need
to happen

Titus 2:5,9

WOMEN AND SLAVES

Don't let Paul's words unnerve you
    women serving husbands
    slaves serving masters
It was a different time
Paul, after all, was human

Search for the underlying Truths
in the Bible
God is kind, merciful, loving
Jesus came to share that Truth
We are all equal in God's eyes

Philemon 1:15-19

AGAINST THE NORM

Paul was not in a position
to abolish slavery
But by opening his heart to God's voice
he may have surprised even himself
when he sent back a runaway slave
with instructions to welcome him
as a brother
Offering to pay for anything he owed

We are not in a position
to abolish every wrong in this world
But by opening our hearts to God's voice
we may surprise even ourselves
when we go against the norm
to welcome those who have hurt us
as our brothers and sisters
Offering to pay for sins with Love

Hebrews 2:17-18

HE KNOWS

Jesus isn't Someone
"out there" or "above us"
He became *one* of us
Sometimes we think of Jesus
as some heavenly creature
who visited us and left

Jesus may have had colds as a kid
probably ran fevers, threw up
Most likely some neighbor kid
hurt His feelings a time or two
Maybe as a teen He had a crush
that was not returned
He was poor, never had wealth
or status or power
When He felt the call to preach
He was often jeered at, driven away
Those in authority plotted against Him
A close friend betrayed Him
He was badly beaten, nails driven
through His hands and feet
His death was agony, torture

When your feelings are hurt
When you are betrayed
When you are sick or in pain
Remember
He knows what it's like
He was not just a "visitor"
He cries for you
        comforts you
                holds you
He Knows
how it feels
to be human
Most importantly
He *chose* to know
for your sake

Hebrews 6:7
DRINK DEEPLY

let God's Word and Love
sink in; drink deeply from it
saturate your soul

Hebrews 8:13
THE NEW COVENANT
OF THE NEW TESTAMENT

We wonder about the violence and sins
—and there were many—
in the Old Testament
Some feel it makes the Bible hypocritical,
                inconsistent, unreliable
Worse, some pick and choose parts and pieces
to justify hateful actions, venomous vengeance

The Old Testament records the history
of ordinary people who made mistakes
who relied on themselves more than God
who did, at times, grasp great insights
                sacrifice for others, listen to our Father
Still, they were people and
people are not perfect

This has to be kept in mind
when reading the Old Testament
Keep in mind, too, that
Jesus is the New Covenant,
                our promise, our hope
He replaces the old ways
with Love, only Love

Hebrews 13:1-5

RULES BY WHICH TO LIVE

So much said in so few lines
a tiny paragraph so easily overlooked
in the enormity of the Bible
Slow up a bit, read carefully
If you do nothing but follow these rules
the rest of your life, you will be a
marvelous example, a testament to
Christianity

Love everyone—even when you'd rather not
        Love the person who cuts you in line
        Love those at home when you're grumpy
Welcome everyone—are you welcoming angels?
        Who knows, but what if you treated
        each person as if he or she were?
Visit prisoners—those held back by bars,
        illness, mental barriers, hopelessness
        Without judging, pretend you are them
Stand up for those who have been wronged
        You are part of one body in Christ
        That mistreated person is you, too
Stay faithful to your partner—that person trusts you
        We all need someone who is on our side
        no matter what happens in our lives
Be content with your blessings—don't obsess over money
        Do your best and trust that God
        will help you in your time of need

Pretty simple, right?
Love and welcome people
Reach out to others and fight for their rights
Honor your soul mate

and

Be content

James 1:13-14

WHEN TEMPTED

God does not tempt us
He does not tempt, test, or trick us

When we are tempted to do something wrong
      it comes from our desires
            to be richer
            to have something someone else has
            to get ahead
            to help ourselves by hurting others

That's on us
God leads us away from temptation
never to it

James 1:22-27

IT'S WHAT WE DO

if you know what God
asks of you, it makes sense to
go out and do it

1 Peter 3:8-11

DO GOOD

Not only have I been tempted
to return insult for insult
I have—gleefully
I become self-righteous
How dare that person judge me!
How dare that person not sing my praises!
How dare that person not see ME but only my flaws!
I stare at my judge with contempt
Complain to loved ones and friends
Shout and swear to make myself feel better

But that's not what Christ did
and He faced much worse than I ever have

Lord, when I am insulted
help me to pray, to decide
if there is some truth
in the accusations, then
learn to be a better person

Lord, when I am insulted,
help me to pray, and
if there is no truth
in the accusations, then
learn to brush aside the insult and still

Do Good

2 Peter 1:19
NIGHT

Right now, it's night

The lamp that helps us see
is the Bible
God's Word

Day will follow

Jesus will return
and be the only Light
we need

Until then
the Bible is our guide
It's confusing, contradictory at times
Yet if we continue to read from its pages
We'll suddenly see a passage or word or story
in a new way
even if we've read that part hundreds of times before

Reading by lamplight is tough
but when
Day dawns

Radiant Light
will fill our hearts and souls
Shining on us
for all time

Then we'll understand

Right now, though, it's night so
I'll light the lamp

1 John 2:9

THE STRUGGLE

Hate slows our steps
   chains our ankles
   adds to our load
Love quickens our pace
   frees us from worry
   lifts our tired hearts
It's a struggle
   to send hate packing
   to give love more room
I'm willing to wrestle hate
   the rest of my life
   if that's what it takes
I'll push hate
   closer to the door
   an inch at a time
One day
   I'll lock it out for good
   and open the windows
To fill my soul
   with pure Light
   Are you with me?

2 John 1:12

FACE TO FACE

We spend so much time
on social media
    Facebook, Twitter, Instagram—
Before I'm done writing this
some new app or site will be waiting

There is nothing wrong with being online
as long as we do it thoughtfully
There is something wrong when we commit
ourselves to cyberspace more than we do
to our family and friends and neighbors

Go out and *live* life, *be* with people
Laugh because you heard someone laugh
and it's contagious—no LOLs
Smile into someone's eyes—no emojis
Put your arms around someone—no "sending" hugs

If you think the virtual life is cool
Wait until you try the real one

3 John 1:2
PROSPERITY

We pray for healthy bodies
for ourselves, for a loved one

How often do we pray
for healthy souls, for faith won?

Jude 1:16
IT'S UP TO YOU

Group One?

Lie, denounce, defy, pounce
Groan, grumble, moan, stumble
Blame, regret, complain, fret

Group Two?

Hope, achieve, cope, believe
Praise, forgive, fill days, live
Pray, raise voice, play, rejoice

Revelation 1:9-20
REVELATION

Now we come to one of the most perplexing books
of the New Testament
You can learn what the numbers
and colors and images symbolize
You can study their meanings
—at least what scholars have interpreted
as their meanings

You can also read it without that knowledge,
letting certain passages
flow into your consciousness
taking from it what you can
leaving the rest for another day
—at least know that it was meant to lend strength
to early Christians and to us

Revelation 2:4-5

GO BACK

For most of us when we first fall in love
We cannot get enough of each other
We are consumed by thoughts of the other
We want only to make that person happy
We don't think about ourselves
We Give

It can be that way when we first believe
We cannot get enough of God's Grace
We are consumed by thoughts of the Light
We want God to be pleased with us
We don't ask for anything
We Give

As we settle into life with our soul mate
We might become complacent
We might become self-centered
Putting ourselves first
Demanding attention
We Take

That can happen with our faith
We forget what a gift this is
We forget the depth of His love
Deciding we've earned this
Justifying actions
We Take

Stop
     Pray
          Breathe

Go back to when you first fell in love
with your soul mate
with your Lord
Go back to the beginning
when you loved completely
and knew love unending

Revelation 7:13-17

TO BE WITH GOD

Our lives on earth
can be tough
For some, even
crushing, devastating

Do your best
Hold tight to your faith
Try to be kind
to those who oppose you

Every bit of heartache
will be forgotten instantly
when God welcomes you
Home ... Protected, Loved

Revelation 8:6-13; 9:1-20
TO FLEE FROM GOD

Trumpet one
One third of the land burned
Trumpet two
One third of sea creatures dead
One third of ships wrecked
Trumpet three
One third of river and spring water poisoned
Trumpet four
One third of the sun and moon darkened
Trumpet five
The torment of locusts turned scorpions
Trumpet six
Four angels riding horses
spewing fire, smoke, sulfur
killing one third of the human race

And those left after all these warnings
refuse to change their ways
murder and rob and commit evil
with no fear of consequences
with no desire to be with God

Revelation 11:15-18
THE SEVENTH TRUMPET

God won't let us clutch
evil forever; the day
of judgment will come

Revelation 12; 13; 14:9-13

TRICKED

Evicted from heaven, the devil was angry
Like a dragon, he tried to destroy Christ
but he couldn't so
He tried to destroy Mary

But he couldn't so
He tried to destroy us
The devil gave authority to a beast
with a fatal wound

Healing the wound was all it took
People were fooled into following the beast
How easy was that?
Then a second beast appeared

and demanded people worship the first beast
And they did
Those who hesitated found life harder so
they followed the beast to ease their suffering

Those who resisted the beast's false claims
were murdered; those people
found final rest, perfect peace
in God

Is this a story?
The end of the world?
Or is it happening now?
Do we recognize when the devil tricks us?

Stay strong
Follow Goodness
Keep your eyes on the
Love and the Light

Revelation 16
THE SEVEN BOWLS

seven more tries to
get our attention, but we
swear at God instead

Revelation 20:1-10
PEACE

Those who are not tricked by the devil
into following the beast
will be given a gift

They alone will live in a world
free from evil
and yet

At the end of one thousand years
of peace
when the devil is released

Some will still be deceived
before God locks the dragon away
forever

Revelation 20:11-15
THE JUDGE

Finally
it will be time—
goodness or crime?

One by one
we will come
before our Father

Revelation 21:1-8, 22-27; 22:1-5
ALL IS NEW

There are no words to describe
what it's like
to live with God
in a place we can't begin to comprehend
A place with no pain, disease, death
A place with no cruelty, hunger, tears
All is new

There are no churches, temples, mosques
No need to seek God
for He lives with us
in a place filled only with Love
A place with Goodness, Light, Truth
A place with Peace, Understanding, Joy
All is new

ABOUT THE POET

Donna Marie Merritt is the author of six previous books of poetry for adults and seventeen books for children. She has written for Christian publications such as *The Word Among Us, The Catholic Yearbook, Signs of the Times, The Catholic Transcript, The Catholic Leader,* and *Liguorian*. Donna holds a certificate in Bible studies from the Archdiocese of Hartford, CT.

CPSIA information can be obtained
at www.ICGtesting.com
Printed in the USA
BVHW081518080820
585841BV00003B/19

9 781945 099250